DEMOCRACY VERSUS EMPIRE

Bernard Semmel is chairman of the history department in the graduate center of the State University of New York at Stony Brook, L.I., New York. He received his B.A. from the College of the City of New York and his M.A. and Ph.D. from Columbia University. He has taught at Queens College in New York, Park College in Missouri, and has been Visiting Professor at Columbia. In addition to DEMOCRACY VERSUS EMPIRE: *The Jamaica Riots of 1865 and the Governor Eyre Controversy*, he has written IMPERIALISM AND SOCIAL REFORM (A618). He has received a Rockefeller Foundation Grant, and has been a Fellow of the American Council of Learned Societies and a Guggenheim Fellow.

BERNARD SEMMEL

———

DEMOCRACY

VERSUS

EMPIRE

The Jamaica Riots of 1865
and the Governor Eyre Controversy

———

This book was previously published
under the title
JAMAICAN BLOOD AND VICTORIAN CONSCIENCE

———

ANCHOR BOOKS
DOUBLEDAY & COMPANY, INC.
GARDEN CITY, NEW YORK
1969

DEMOCRACY VERSUS EMPIRE: *The Jamaica Riots of 1865 and the Governor Eyre Controversy* was originally published by MacGibbon & Kee Ltd. in 1962 under the title *The Governor Eyre Controversy* and in 1963 by Houghton Mifflin Company under the title *Jamaican Blood and Victorian Conscience* with subtitle "The Governor Eyre Controversy." The Anchor Books edition is published by arrangement with MacGibbon & Kee Ltd.

Anchor Books edition: 1969

FOR MAXINE

FOREWORD

The controversy growing out of the Jamaica uprising of 1865 gripped the interest of contemporaries, and has been frequently mentioned by historians of Victorian thought. Yet there has been no extended study of the incident. This narrative essay, though not a definitive treatment, attempts to tell the story of the controversy, and to fit it into its historic setting. The nature of the subject has persuaded me to forego the use of footnotes, and to rely instead upon a selected bibliography.

The book was undertaken several years ago as a respite during the course of work upon another book, since published, of a rather different character, and concerned with the politics and ideas of a later generation of Englishmen; the two books, nonetheless, share a common general theme—the interdependence of British imperial and domestic politics. The specific theme of the present work is whether the maintenance of a colonial empire is compatible with liberal democracy within the metropolis. The book, no doubt, betrays at least two prejudices: a grudging admiration for the British Empire, and a more freely given, though qualified, admiration for the brand of liberalism whose spokesman was John Stuart Mill. The story of the Eyre controversy presents the two—the empire and Mill's liberalism—in conflict; a great achievement of British politics has been that the conflict was not to prove irreconcilable.

The book profited from the suggestions of a number of persons, at various stages of the writing. Among them have been my present colleagues, Professor Richard M. Morse, and Mr Daniel Gasman; and Mr Melvin Landsberg. I am again indebted to Professor D. V. Glass of the London School of Economics for his advice and encouragement. I should also like to thank Mr John Buchanan of the Cornell University Library for his aid in connection with the Goldwin Smith papers.

My wife has lived with this manuscript, in its various stages, for some time, and has typed more than one draft. Without her counsel and encouragement, it would not have been written. This book is dedicated to her.

BERNARD SEMMEL

New York, January 1962

CONTENTS

FOREWORD   7

PROLOGUE   11

   I   'Massacre': Exeter Hall Demands an Inquiry   13

  II   Governor Eyre, Jamaica and Insurrection   28

 III   The Jamaica Committee and Parliament: J. S. Mill   58

 IV   'Reform', Southampton, and Charles Kingsley   85

  V   The Gladiators: Carlyle and Ruskin v. Darwin and Huxley   107

 VI   The Constitution, the 'Rabble' and the Empire   134

VII   The Prosecution   149

EPILOGUE   180

SELECTED BIBLIOGRAPHY   190

INDEX   197

PROLOGUE

In October 1865, there took place an uprising of Negro
peasantry upon the island-colony of Jamaica, in the
British West Indies. The uprising was speedily suppressed
by troops under the direction of the colonial governor, Edward Eyre. In the course of the pacification of the island
by the army, during a month-long reign of terror, a thousand homes were burnt, nearly five hundred Negroes were
killed, and more than that number were flogged and
tortured. While restoring order, Governor Eyre had managed to secure the court martial and execution of a personal
and political enemy, a mulatto member of the Jamaica
House of Assembly. The story of the insurrection and its
repression was broadcast throughout the civilized world
during the last months of 1865. Nowhere was there more
horror and agitation than in England itself. A contemporary journalist, Justin McCarthy, reported that:

> For some weeks there was hardly anything talked of,
> we might almost say hardly anything thought of, in
> England, but the story of the rebellion that had taken
> place in the island of Jamaica, and the manner in which
> it had been suppressed and punished. . . .
> The history of the events in Jamaica, told in what-
> ever way, must form a sad and shocking narrative. The
> history of this generation has no such tale to tell where
> any race of civilized and Christian men was concerned.

Had the repression been justifiable in all its details; had the fearful vengeance taken on the wretched island been absolutely necessary to its future tranquility, it still would have been a chapter in history to read with a shudder.

The Jamaica insurrection gave rise to a three-year long controversy as to whether Governor Eyre ought to be treated as a hero who had saved Jamaica for the Crown, and the lives of 13,000 white men and women in the bargain, or whether his repression of the uprising had revealed him as not only stupid, cruel, and incompetent, but a murderer. In 1866, 1867, and 1868, both houses of parliament resounded more than once to eloquent debate upon this question; the press took sides which admitted no middle ground; riots and street brawls marked the progress of events; England's leading men of letters and of science took active positions in the controversy, and the closely knit world of mid-Victorian science and letters saw the straining of close friendships. It is the story of the controversy set into motion by these events in Jamaica, and its meaning, which we will tell, for, as Leonard Huxley has written, the Eyre case 'became the touchstone of ultimate political convictions.'

1

'MASSACRE':
EXETER HALL DEMANDS AN
INQUIRY

The first news of the Jamaica insurrection had come to
England in the bundles of Kingston newspapers which had
come aboard the West-India mail-packet in November
1865. The planter journals wrote hysterically of the prospect of a slaughter of the white population of the island
such as had occurred at Haiti over half a century earlier.
The passengers aboard the packet added stories of savageries committed by the rebellious blacks, from which
they accounted themselves most fortunate to have es-
caped. Upon closer questioning, it turned out that none
of these persons had actually witnessed the atrocities of
which they spoke, and much of the British public tended
rather to discount the tales of their Creole cousins. Yet,
Jamaica had long been a troubled island, had, indeed,
been the scene of a number of past insurrections during
the period before the emancipation of the slaves, none of
which, however, had approached the Haitian experience.
It was therefore difficult to believe that thirty years after
emancipation, Jamaica's black men, so often charged with
an indolent apathy, would erupt in so terrifying a manner.
What did disturb a good part of the English public was
the bloodthirstiness of the chatter of the packet's passengers. The language of the Kingston newspapers, too, ex-
ulting in the work of revenge, lovingly depicting the reign
of terror initiated by Her Majesty's forces against the
rebels—picturing in detail the hangings, floggings, and

burnings of homes—and applauding the brutal suppression
of the enemies of the Queen—a lesson the confounded
blacks would not soon forget—was a cause for concern.
Yet, Englishmen preferred to think that the Jamaican
newspapers had exaggerated the work of suppression just
as they had, the public felt confident, the facts of the
insurrection itself.

A few days after these first tidings, the report of the
Governor of Jamaica, Edward Eyre, appended to which
were the reports of British military commanders in the
field, arrived at the Colonial Office and were immediately
published to satisfy an intense public curiosity. These
served to confirm the wildest rantings of the Jamaican
press—at least so far as the terrible suppression of the
revolt was concerned—and the worst suspicions of English
humanitarians. The reports of one officer, a Colonel Hobbs,
caused special concern. For example:

(19th October 1865): I found a number of special constables, who had captured a number of prisoners from
the rebel camp. Finding their guilt clear, and being
unable to either take or leave them, I had them all
shot. The constables then hung them up on trees—eleven
in number. Their countenances were all diabolical, and
they never flinched the very slightest. From this we at
once went to Stony Gut, and to be brief, can only say
that had the rebels been brave and met us there, not a
man of the 6th Regiment would have returned to tell
the tale.

(19th October 1865): I must not forget to tell you that
I have Paul Bogle's valet for my guide, a little fellow
of extraordinary intelligence, a light rope tied to the
stirrup, and a revolver now and then to his head, causes
us thoroughly to understand each other, and he knows
every single rebel in the Island by name and face, and
has just been selecting the captains, colonels and sec-
retaries out of an immense gang of prisoners just come
in here whom I shall have to shoot tomorrow morning.

English newspaper readers were greatly upset at this method for establishing guilt or innocence. The other commanders in the field had similar stories to tell. The statement following came from the report of a Captain Hole:

(17th October 1865): On arriving yesterday at Long Bay I found the huts full of plunder. I had every house within a quarter of a mile of the road in which plunder was found fired, and in doing so upwards of twenty of the rebels were killed. . . . Within a mile of us every black man who did not stand at our approach to give an account of himself was shot. . . . I am of opinion that upwards of sixty rebels were killed yesterday by the troops under my command, among whom I hear there are some ring leaders. . . . I intend to have destroyed all houses in which proved rebels have resided.

Lieutenant Adcock reported to his commanding officer:

I visited several estates and villages. I burnt seven houses in all, but did not even see a rebel. On returning to Golden Grove in the evening, sixty-seven prisoners had been sent in. . . . I disposed of as many as possible, but was too tired to continue after dark. . . .

From the fatigued Lieutenant Adcock, we turn to Captain Ford:

We made a raid with thirty men; flogging nine men and burning their negro houses. We held a court martial on the prisoners, who amounted to about fifty or sixty. Several were flogged without court martial, from a simple examination.

Captain Ford good humouredly summarized in conclusion:

This is a picture of martial law. The soldiers enjoy it, the inhabitants here dread it. If they run on their approach, they are shot for running away.

The middle-class Radicals who had been horrified by less serious atrocities in Central or Eastern Europe were indignant at such happenings under the British flag. Much of the London press was vehement in its denunciation of this brutality. Nor was Governor Eyre spared, despite his excellent reputation for fair dealing with the darker races. Particular attention was paid to Eyre's account of the court martial of George William Gordon, a mulatto member of the Jamaican House of Assembly, and the alleged leader of the revolt. From Eyre's report, his trial had been marked by a number of serious irregularities. It was with such prompting that Secretary for the Colonies Cardwell, on November 23rd, sent a dispatch to Jamaica asking the Governor to send copies of all the court martial proceedings at Morant Bay, particularly the documents and evidence pertinent to the Gordon case. The Governor was informed that Her Majesty's government awaited 'with much anxiety' his explanations: 'I desire also to see it clear established,' Cardwell wrote, 'that he was not executed until crimes had been proved in evidence against him which deserved death; and that the prompt infliction of capital punishment was necessary to rescue the colony from imminent danger, and from the horrors of a general or widespread insurrection, and the repetition elsewhere of such a slaughter of the white and coloured colonists as had taken place in the eastern part of the island.' The professional officials at the Colonial Office were not behind their Secretary in recognizing the gravity of the situation. Eyre had for many years been a special favourite of Frederic Rogers, the Permanent Under-Secretary, who had supported him in the face of some previous opposition. Now, however, Rogers realized that the Governor had overstepped the bounds of discretion. In a letter to his sister, on 25th November 1865, Rogers related:

We are expecting our Jamaica news with some anxiety. The soldiers seem to have made wildish work of it, and Eyre's hanging a member of the Assembly by court

martial, sending him from Kingston for the purpose is
rather startling. . . .

After further news was received from Jamaica, Rogers
wrote:

> The Jamaica business is most terrible. The doings on
> both sides appear in truth to be rather worse than
> better than what you see in the papers. . . . It is really
> terrible to see human nature naked.

One section of the public reacted with a spontaneous
unanimity—the societies of the largely middle-class, dissenting, non-conforming sects: the Baptists, Congregation-
alists, Methodists, Quakers, and Unitarians. Before awaiting Eyre's explanations or impartial inquiries, these
dissenting groups—known collectively as 'Exeter Hall'
from their headquarters off the Strand—denounced Eyre
and the barbarities committed by British troops in Jamaica, and commenced a campaign for retribution. Exeter
Hall was set into action by its deeply entrenched,
philanthropic vested interests on behalf of the 'lesser'
races which predetermined its point of view in all matters
of this kind. Although the dissenting sects differed widely
in theology, they were closely united in their political and
humanitarian efforts, and wealthy Dissenters, who made
handsome contributions to foreign missionary efforts, regarded themselves as the special protectors of the newly
baptised—or even of pagans who constituted a potential
'market' for salvation. To many Englishmen, Exeter Hall's
intensive missionary activities revealed a distorted sense of
values—this bother with heathen souls overseas while there
was so much to be done at home, so many native British
souls to be saved. But the Hall had a taste for the exotic.
Following the pattern set by much of English industry,
Exeter Hall was interested in Christianity for export. The
Negro Christians of Jamaica had been the special protégés
of English non-conformist missionaries. How could Exeter
Hall tolerate the hanging and whipping of its spiritual
wards—of men and women upon whom it had bestowed

an immortal soul; even the long campaign against slavery which had led to emancipation in 1833 had been directed by non-conformity and Evangelicalism.

Exeter Hall's special interest in the Negro freedmen of the Indies had been noted and denounced some fifteen years before the Jamaica troubles by Thomas Carlyle, in his 'Occasional Discourse on the Nigger Question,' in *Fraser's Magazine* for December 1849, which was cast into the form of a speech to an imaginary Universal Abolition-of-Pain Association, located, of course, in Exeter Hall. In the West Indies, the speaker reported, 'Exeter Hall has had its way'—the slaves were free. 'Sitting yonder with their beautiful muzzles up to the ears in pumpkins, imbibing sweet pulps and juices; the grinder and incisor teeth ready for every new work, and the pumpkins cheap as grass in those rich climates: while the sugar crops rot . . . because labour cannot be hired, so cheap are the pumpkins.' This was a consequence of the 'rose-pink sentimentalism' of Exeter Hall and of 'philanthropic Liberalism.' 'Quashee,' Carlyle continued, 'if he will not help in bringing out the spices, will get himself made a slave again (which state will be a little less ugly than his present one), and with beneficent whip, since other methods avail not, will be compelled to work.' Carlyle's attack upon humanitarian philanthropy prompted John Stuart Mill to reply in the next issue of *Fraser's*. Mill protested Carlyle's reliance on the 'old law of the strongest,' 'the law of force and cunning; the law that whoever is more powerful than another, is "born lord" of that other, the other being born his "servant,"' and attacked Carlyle's 'gospel of work' by setting up his 'gospel of leisure.'

The news from Jamaica reminded Exeter Hall of its fight against Rajah James Brooke. About the time of the Mill-Carlyle exchange in 1849, the Anti-Slavery Society and the Aborigines Protection Society, the eyes and ears of Exeter Hall, were turning their attention to Malaya and to Rajah Brooke. Because of Brooke's services in helping to suppress a rebellion, the Sultan of Brunei had appointed him Rajah of Sarawak on the island of Borneo in 1842. At the same time he received an appointment as the British consul in the region. It was an unlikely combination, and Brooke appears to have used his British consulship, and British naval units, to further the tribal aspirations of his Sarawakian subjects. When this news reached England, there was an outcry from Exeter Hall and the middle-class Radicals to protest this abuse of British power. The Russell government and its Foreign Secretary, Viscount Palmerston, stood behind Brooke, but in 1854, the government of Lord Aberdeen finally agreed to hold a board of inquiry, which vindicated Brooke's conduct but undermined his authority. Brooke enjoyed wide support in England, and when he visited London in the midst of the agitation in 1852, he was the honoured guest at a dinner given for him by some of the leading figures in British public life. In 1855, for example, Charles Kingsley published *Westward Ho!*, a story of the Elizabethan sea-dogs, and dedicated the book to Brooke.

The news from Jamaica also reminded Exeter Hall of a more recent occasion when it had ignominiously failed to do battle for its principles—the celebrated Indian mutiny. A kindly view of the native races had taken a strong hold upon the British public early in the century, but this view was being whittled away by the apparently ceaseless wars which Britain was waging against coloured peoples, as part of their operations to safeguard what England already possessed and to extend commerce and the area of colonization. The fighting with the New Zealand Maori, for example, was still raging fiercely when the news of the Jamaican atrocities reached England and the Maori war had been in progress for over five years by 1865. Such wars could not help but have a cumulative effect upon the way in which the British public regarded the coloured peoples under their rule, and in the course of the years, these 'natives' came to be thought of as bloodthirsty savages rather than peaceful children of nature. This view was almost ineradicably fixed upon the collective mind of the British public by the events of the Indian Mutiny of 1857. Day after day, the newspapers told stories of massacres of British women and children, of gruesome oriental tortures and mutilations, of assaults on the virtue and honour of

English women. Reports were received of aristocratic
English ladies dragged naked through the streets of Delhi
and exhibited to the lecherous gaze of its senile King. The
outcry was instantaneous. A demand for vengeance was
heard on all sides. The Whig parliamentarian and historian, Thomas Babington Macaulay, wrote in his diary,
in June 1857:

> The cruelties of the Sepoy natives have inflamed the
> Nation to a degree unprecedented within my memory.
> Peace Societies, Aborigines Protection Societies, and
> societies for the reformation of criminals are silent. There
> is one terrible cry to revenge. . . . The almost universal
> feeling is that not a single Sepoy within the walls of
> Delhi should be spared, and I own that is a feeling with
> which I cannot help sympathizing.

The mutiny was finally suppressed in just this spirit. No
quarter was given to murderers, mutilators, and violators
of British womankind. After vengeance had been taken, it
was discovered—all too late—that the stories of Sepoy
atrocities had been enormously exaggerated. For the comparatively few Englishmen who had indeed been killed,
a terrible ransom was exacted. After the capture of Delhi,
innocent citizens were clubbed to death or bayonetted as
they pleaded for mercy. One eye witness reported that
'the very sight of a dark man stimulated our national en-
thusiasm almost to frenzy.' A gallows was set up in a city
square and hundreds of innocent Indians were hanged as
drunken British soldiers laughingly watched the death
struggles of their convulsing corpses. What was more
horrible was the general taste for blood exhibited by the
British public which rejoiced in the stories of the terrible
vengeance, and derided the efforts of the Governor-
General, Lord Canning, to restrain the frenzy, denouncing
him with the name of 'Clemency Canning.' Was it to be
wondered at that British officials and soldiers in Jamaica
in 1865 might strain to avoid such a sobriquet? The Mutiny
and its repression served to further prepare Englishmen

to accept any action on the part of strong rulers and
administrators to stamp out colonial disorder.

When the Jamaica news came rushing in upon England,
Exeter Hall and Louis Chamerovzow, who was virtually its
executive director in matters of this sort, were prepared for
action. Through many years, by his forthright stands in
defence of coloured peoples, Louis Chamerovzow's name
had become known throughout the Empire, and his reputation was such that when a native felt oppressed by a
colonial official, he frequently complained not to the
Colonial Secretary but to Chamerovzow. Before being
hung, Gordon, the alleged leader of the Jamaica insurrection, instructed his wife to inform Chamerovzow of the
preceedings. It was Chamerovzow—one journal described
him as 'a Polish gentleman who kindly superintends English philanthropy'—who typified the protective attitude
which Exeter Hall displayed towards the coloured races
and he—like the Hall itself—came in for much disparage-
ment.

The Hall denounced Governor Eyre just as it had denounced Rajah Brooke, and how much more enthusiasti-
cally it could fight for the black Baptists and Methodists of
Jamaica than for the brown Hindus and Mussulmen of
India! The execution of Gordon, who had been a lay
Baptist preacher, was compared by Exeter Hall orators to
the martyrdom of St Stephen. The societies which Carlyle
had collectively denounced as the universal Abolition-Of-
Pain Association again had a cause after their own heart,
and were determined to fight it through.

One of the first newspapers to report on the suppression
of the troubles at Morant Bay was the sensationalist *New
York Herald,* which had headlined its story:

'Eight Miles of Dead Bodies.'

By the end of November, dissenting groups had placarded
London with the legend, 'Eight Miles of Dead Bodies.'
Further explanation was not necessary. Everyone was dis-

cussing the events in Jamaica, and taking one position or the other. While the Radical *Morning Star* stressed the atrocities committed against the Negroes by British troops, the weekly *News of the World* wrote only of Negro 'savageries' against whites. During the first two weeks in December, 1865, the Colonial Office was besieged by delegations demanding Governor Eyre's immediate removal from office. The most imposing of these, consisting of over 250 gentlemen of the British and Foreign Anti-Slavery Society, came, on Saturday, December 9th, to present a memorial to Colonial Secretary Cardwell. Included in the delegation were the wealthy Nottingham hosierer, lay Congregationalist leader, and M.P., Samuel Morley; the son of the leader of the parliamentary fight for emancipation, Sir Thomas Fowell Buxton; the noted Quaker banker, who was president of the Anti-Slavery Society, Samuel Gurney; and, of course, Louis Chamerovzow. When Buxton asked Cardwell that Eyre be immediately suspended, a member of the delegation shouted, 'Yes, by the neck,' amid ripples of assent. Thomas Hughes, a Radical barrister and author, who had recently been elected a member of parliament for Lambeth, joined the delegation in denouncing Eyre. He spoke, Hughes declared, 'as an Englishman, jealous of the honour of England,' which had been placed in jeopardy by the Government of Jamaica. The Colonial Secretary listened in silence. When everyone had spoken, he assured them that an inquiry certainly must and would take place; he added, however, that, although he did not know the Governor personally, he knew him by his reputation as a 'man of courage and humanity,' and sympathized with the difficulties of Eyre's position. Members of the delegation protested, but the interview was concluded.

A few days after the reception of the mammoth delegation from the Anti-Slavery Society, the London Missionary Society called upon Cardwell, who received them in the company of the Prime Minister, Earl Russell. After listening to its request that Eyre be suspended, the Prime Minister replied with, as he put it, 'the deepest pain on very many accounts.' 'Considering how long it is since the abolition of slavery,' Russell continued, 'it was to be hoped that the condition of Society there would by this time have become one of harmony and good feeling between the different races, and it is to be deeply regretted that it should still be one of so much ill-will, complaint, and difficulty on the one side, and of complaint, discontent and dissipation on the other.' The Prime Minister concluded by requesting the deputation not to underestimate, as they certainly seemed to be doing, the gravity of the rising at Morant Bay.

These memorials by delegations of church and philanthropic societies were underscored by more raucous shoutings from mass meetings. In late November, there was a meeting at Manchester, with the Mayor of that city in the chair and Jacob Bright, the brother of the political leader of Radicalism, John Bright, as the principal speaker. The Tory *Saturday Review* described the gathering in unfriendly terms, adding that to politicians of Bright's school 'every rebel is a hero or a victim, and a guardian of order, even when he acts in self-defence, is guilty of lawless violence.' In early December, a similar mass-meeting was held in the seacoast town of Brighton. The blind Henry Fawcett, the political economist and a newly elected Liberal M.P., spoke of the 'terrible slaughter' which had taken place in Jamaica as 'a barbarity which never occurred in the time of the blackest pages of history.' Working men's protest gatherings took place. The British working-class had in the past demonstrated its sympathy with the 'suppressed' nationalities, with the Poles, the Magyars, and the Italians, and now extended its sympathy to Jamaican blacks. Friedrich Engels, writing to Karl Marx in London, on November 17, 1865, asked: 'Was sagst du zu der Nigger-insurrektion auf Jamaika und den Brutalitäten der Engländer?' and Marx replied three days later that 'Die Jamaika geschichte für die Hundsgemeinheit des "true Englishman" charakteristisch. Die Kerls haben den Russen nichts vorzuwerfen.'

Mary Eyre, the Governor's sister, wrote to the Radical *Morning Star*, which had taken a lead in denouncing the Governor, protesting that 'It is not fair, Sir, it is not English, to publish only letters abusing a man and stigmatizing him as "a wholesale murderer and a Robespierre," who ought to be hung with the same rope with which he hung Gordon, and none in his defence.' She loyally defended her brother's conduct in Jamaica and lauded him as a good and kind brother. 'Amid all his hard work,' she wrote, 'he found time to write a brief letter home to me enclosing £50 to pay for the schooling of a little niece whose parents are far from rich.' The *Star* published her letter. The following day Miss Eyre received two anonymous letters and one unsigned telegram which she hastened to make public as an indication of the low spirit of the enemies of her brother. One of the letters read:

Madam,

You have done a smart thing, no doubt, trying to defend your bloody, murderous brother, who deserves a rope if every anyone did, and I hope he will get it.

That £50 you speak of makes his character even blacker. It is stolen goods; plunder from the poor blacks. A greater scoundrel never walked the earth, and to help him he got the bloody Nelson and others to work and 'rum'd' the sailors that they might cut up the poor, because they are black and coloured.

The curse of the nation and world will ever rest upon your family for these bloody crimes. Bloody cries for vengeance upon you all.

The telegram was necessarily more succinct:

MADAM—I HAVE READ YOUR SILLY LETTER AND JUST AS SURE AS YOUR DASTARD OF A BROTHER MURDERED POOR MR GORDON HE SHALL SWING FOR IT AT THE OLD BAILEY.

The *Pall Mall Gazette* could only write that the cry raised against Eyre seemed 'so brutal and so senseless that one might almost suppose that it was raised by far-sighted friends who hoped that the disgust which it is calculated to excite, would in due time be converted into sympathy for the person against whom it is directed.'

Governor Eyre was not without defenders. One of his earliest supporters was Lord Elcho, a Scottish Whig member of the lower house who, at this time, was one of the foremost opponents of electoral reform. Over five years previously, Elcho had been a chief sponsor of the Volunteers—trained citizen soldiers, drawn mostly from the middle classes, who participated in regular training sessions so as to be ready to fight upon call. Elcho was particularly proud of the gallant conduct of the Volunteers of Jamaica. In a speech at a dinner of the United East Lothian Agricultural Society on December 4th, Elcho told how his blood boiled whenever he read articles or speeches by 'a small but noisy' portion of the community about Jamaica. These people (in a letter to *The Times* a retired Rear-Admiral who also defended the Governor called 'these people' the 'Manchester clique') sat in their homes, in safe and comfortable arm chairs, and judged the actions of their compatriots exposed to the greatest dangers in Jamaica! These arm-chair heroes dared to call fine, brave men cowards and murderers. Was that fitting reward for their valiant action in saving a valuable possession of the Crown and the lives of thirteen thousand whites on the island?

The same tack was taken in a letter to a newspaper, signed, simply, 'A White Man':

I venture to appeal to you [the letter read] for some sympathy with white men. At present the Baptists and Wesleyans seem bent on exterminating people who have the misfortune to be born white. Last night, at Exeter Hall, the onslaught on us poor whites was terrible.

The letter went on to denounce this 'maudlin sentimentality,' adding that the black should 'be made to work or left to starve if he prefers idleness.' The 'White Man' refused to believe that 'Exeter Hall is the true House of Assembly, and that Governor Eyre has been superseded by Governor Gurney.' The weekly magazine, *Punch,* quite early in the affair became a staunch supporter of Eyre.

A poem, in that journal, called 'Two Sides to the Question: A Hint to Exeter Hall' read:

> *Does human kindness drain its cup*
> *For black and whitey-brown,*
> *That still you cry the darky up*
> *And bowl the planter down?*

Lord Melville expressed his sorrow 'that the Governor's conduct should be subject to review by men who never knew what danger was.'

At first it had only been the enemies of Eyre who demanded an inquiry. After much agitation, even those who supported the Governor insisted upon an inquiry, as, in justice, due to him in view of all the 'slander' raised against him. The much-respected London *Times* took the lead and called for a searching investigation and while urging that there be no prejudgment of the case, added:

> The man who has been denounced as 'a wholesale murderer' and a 'Robespierre' is the same man who was protector of the aborigines in South Australia, and who distinguished himself by the defence of the very principles which he is now charged with outraging. He is also a man who, by the admission of his detractors, has given as high proofs of courage as any other man alive, and who, therefore, was eminently unlikely to lose his nerve for a fortnight or three weeks together under the pressure of an emergency, however terrible.

The *Pall Mall Gazette* joined in advising the Nation: 'Let a man at all events be tried before he is hanged, especially if his alleged crime is that of hanging people before he tried them.'

Meanwhile, at Kingston, Governor Edward Eyre was blissfully unaware of the great controversy in progress in England. He could only assume that he was regarded as much a hero in England as he was in Jamaica. On that island, all previous hostility towards him—and there had been considerable—had been forgotten. He had been forgiven everything. The whites of Jamaica could think of him now only as the man who had saved them from the fate of Haiti. When Eyre received Cardwell's first dispatch to him, conveying satisfaction, he was delighted. He took full pride in the congratulations which Cardwell had heaped upon him for his promptness in suppressing the insurrection, but in Cardwell's subsequent request for further explanation, he sensed a sign of displeasure. Therefore, when, on December 8th, he answered the Colonial Secretary to thank him for his congratulations, he claimed general ignorance as to what had happened in the field, pleading the pressure of events. No longer did he accept full responsibility, as he had in an earlier dispatch, a responsibility he now placed upon Brigadier General Nelson in the districts east of Morant Bay, and upon Colonel Hobbs in the district north-west of the Bay.

Before Eyre's letter of reply could reach London, the Colonial Office had decided that a commission of inquiry had to be appointed, and Cardwell wrote Eyre of the Colonial Office's decision to temporarily relieve him of all authority during the course of the inquiry and to give gubernatorial power and title to the presiding officer of the Royal Commission of Inquiry. Cardwell further explained in his dispatch:

Whilst we feel it to be our imperative duty to institute this inquiry, we desire by every means in our power to guard against in any way prejudging its result. Our earnest hope is that the result will be to satisfy us on the points on which it is necessary for us to be satisfied, and at the same time to exhibit the conduct of those whose duty has compelled them to take part in these proceedings, and to whom the repression of the outbreak has been due, in a light which may show it to have been consistent with their position and character, and especially in your own case, with that high character for courage and for humanity by which you have always been distinguished.

2

GOVERNOR EYRE, JAMAICA AND INSURRECTION

In the midst of the Jamaica controversy—in the summer of 1867—the secretary of the Eyre Defence Committee, an Australian residing in London named Alexander Hamilton Hume, wrote a biography of the Governor which painted him in glowing colours, though ineptly supplying ammunition for his enemies. From Hume's account, we learn that Edward Eyre's grandfather had served as the Canon of York Cathedral, and his father, also a clergyman, had had several cures in the East Riding of Yorkshire, in one of which the future Governor of Jamaica was born. Eyre was a third son but his two elder brothers had died as children and consequently he had been treated with special care. Hume related stories of Eyre's childhood as early evidence of his hero's daring and courage. For example, at least twice young Edward had jumped into rivers out of which he had to be humiliatingly fished, not being able to swim. On another occasion, young Edward had climbed to the top of a tall tree, had then discovered that he could not descend, and was obliged to wait on a branch for hours, before rescuers arrived with ladders. Eyre's enemies were to see in both these stories neither courage nor daring but an early revelation of the future Colonial Governor's lack of good sense. Edward was not a scholar. Some of his teachers, his admiring biographer related, considered his memory 'defective,' but he was fond of carpentry and fishing. The natural career for such a young gentleman was either the Church or the Army, and he had preferred the Army. Although Eyre's father had a 'good cure,' it took some years to amass the £400 necessary to buy a commission but the clergyman managed. One can imagine the elder Eyre's hurt surprise when his son informed him that he had changed his mind. Edward had decided to go as a settler to Australia and proposed to take the £400 to give himself a start. His father was naturally shocked that his son should want the hard-saved money for a 'speculation,' but Edward was determined, and, at the age of seventeen, with £400 and some letters of introduction in his pocket, the youngster set sail for Sydney.

The Australian gamble proved successful. There was something about the new environment which brought forth the best in the young man. Within a few years, Eyre had become a well-to-do and highly respected sheepraiser in South Australia, and had been appointed Resident Magistrate for the Murray River Territory. In his conduct of that office he had revealed himself so tactful in his handling of the Australian natives and so considerate of their rights, that he had been appointed 'Protector of the Aborigines.' As 'Protector,' he made a reputation for himself as a friend of the Australian black-fellows. By 1840, his youthful energies once more called for action and he undertook to head an expedition to explore unknown parts of the Australian continent. The expedition was small and its difficulties over desolate terrain in a hard Australian winter were many. After over a year in the wilderness, Eyre returned to civilization as the only white survivor of the journey, and was immediately acclaimed the hero of Southern and Western Australia, and remains so to this day.

Eyre wrote a book about this expedition, which received considerable notice in England during the 'forties,' and in which he made himself a leading advocate of the rights of the Australian native races. A younger brother of the clergyman-writer, Charles Kingsley—Henry Kingsley—who was later to serve as one of the most active members of the Eyre Defence Committee, wrote an article on

Governor Eyre's Australian explorations which, with odd
timing, appeared, in *Macmillan's Magazine*, in October
1865, just a few weeks before the trouble at Morant Bay.
Wrote Kingsley:

> No man concealed less than Eyre the vices of the na-
> tives; but no man stood more steadfastly in the breach
> between them and the squatters (the great pastoral
> aristocracy) at a time when to do so was social ostra-
> cism. . . . He pleaded for the black, and tried to stop
> the war of extermination which was, is, and I suppose
> will be, carried on by the colonists against the natives
> in the unsettled districts beyond the reach of the public
> eye. His task was hopeless. It was easier for him to find
> water in the desert than to find mercy for the savages.
> Honour to him for attempting it, however.

In 1845, after twelve years in Australia, Eyre returned to
England, taller and heavier, and wearing a full beard. He
brought with him two native boys whom he took to Buck-
ingham Palace to see Queen Victoria and Prince Albert.
The dramatic gesture, underlining his successes in Australia, attracted the favourable notice of the Colonial
Office. In so many colonies, the Colonial Office had been
constantly bothered by the difficulties of keeping the
peace between white settlers and natives, so that a respected settler who sympathized with the natives was a
genuine find. In 1846, Eyre was rewarded by an appointment as Lieutenant-Governor of New Zealand.

Eyre's activities in New Zealand attracted favourable
attention. Both New Zealand's Governor-in-Chief, Sir
George Grey and the Colonial Secretary set him down
as possessing both 'zeal and intelligence.' After six years,
he returned to England with his family in September 1853,
and, a year later, his old chief in New Zealand, Sir George
Grey, who was at this time the Secretary of State for the
Colonies, appointed him Lieutenant-Governor of the island of St Vincent in the West Indies, an office he held
for six years, until the end of March 1861.

Up to this point, Eyre's career had been most successful. He had entirely satisfied the Governors of the Colonies under whom he had served, and the Colonial Office thought well of him. Indeed, a twentieth-century British Governor of Jamaica, after reviewing confidential colonial office files, has declared that Eyre was a protected pet of the colonial office bureaucracy. Thus far, his experience had been limited to service in subordinate capacities, but Sir Frederic Rogers, the chief of the permanent staff of the colonial office, and Eyre's particular friend, was anxious that he should have his chance. In the early part of 1862, the Colonial Secretary, the Duke of Newcastle, at the suggestion of Rogers, commissioned Eyre to administer, temporarily, the government-in-chief of Jamaica and its dependencies during the absence of its regular governor, William Darling. Jamaica was one of the leading colonies and its governorship, even though temporary, was an important and a most troublesome post. Newcastle had doubts as to whether Eyre's experience were sufficient to enable him to handle so difficult an assignment—but agreed to the appointment since it was felt that Governor Darling would soon return.

In the eighteenth century, Englishmen considered the sugar island of Jamaica one of the bright jewels in the imperial crown. In the following century, it was regarded as one of the burdens of the empire, rather than one of its blessings. Jamaica is the largest island in the British West Indies—about fifty miles wide at its widest point and about three times as long, comprising nearly 4,500 square miles in all. The beautiful Blue Mountains range from its western to its eastern tip. Most of the island is a white limestone plateau, broken by steep hills, deep valleys, and sharp gulleys. Upon the long plain on the southern coast are the cities of Spanish Town and Kingston. In 1865, Spanish Town was the seat of government, while bustling Kingston was the largest city and the capital. The island colony lies about eighty miles south of the eastern tip of Cuba, and, until the middle of the seventeenth century, had belonged to Spain. The Spaniards had succeeded in destroying the native Arawak Indians during their long

rule. The Arawaks, unaccustomed to the forced labour on
Spanish plantations, had been worn down by disease and
the humiliation of serfdom, and Negro slaves had to be
imported from Africa to work the fields. When Oliver
Cromwell's admirals captured the island in 1655, its total
population was under 3,000. More slaves were imported
by the English and—almost from the founding of the
Royal Africa Company in 1672 onward—Jamaica became
one of the great slave markets of the world. When the
slave trade was abolished in 1807, Jamaica had about
320,000 slaves working its sugar fields, growing its coffee,
cocoa, indigo, and cultivating such spices as pimento and
ginger.

The nineteenth century was not to be kind to the island. In the decades following the Napoleonic wars, the
Jamaican economy was being profoundly altered, although
the Colonial Office in London, and its Governors in Jamaica preferred to ignore the changing circumstances.
First of all, Jamaica had always been a rather high-cost
producer of sugar, and the opening of better sugar lands
in Cuba and Brazil and, in addition, the growing competition of the new, highly subsidized, European beet sugar,
depressed the world sugar price and, in the Jamaican
phrase, 'ruinated' many sugar plantations upon the island.
The end of slavery—making necessary a painful adjustment to a free labour system—and the end of preferential
treatment for Jamaican sugar in the British market, with
the coming of free trade in the 1840's, severely compli-
cated an already difficult situation.

With slave emancipation, many of the freedmen left
the great sugar estates, where their former masters were
offering pittance wages, and settled upon unoccupied
lands in the hills. Despite planter-inspired legislation to
discourage these settlements, they increased and pros-
pered. By 1860, there were approximately 50,000 small
landowners in the hills, producing such provision crops as
yams, breadfruit, and plantains for local consumption, and
ginger, pimento, and coffee for export. The British government, unfortunately, like Carlyle in his diatribe of 1849,
preferred to think of this development not as a healthy

adjustment to the decaying Jamaica sugar economy, nor as a natural reaction to the existence of large areas of un-occupied land. Rather, they bemoaned the fact that the lazy Quashee preferred to grow his own food rather than work for the low, irregular and uncertain wages of the frequently absentee estate owners.

During the 'fifties and 'sixties, conditions became worse, nor was any action taken to better them. The pressure of competition from the low-cost, slave-grown sugar of Cuba and Brazil continued to undermine the estate economy. Furthermore, the years preceding the uprising of 1865 were marked by frequent droughts falling hard upon the settlers in the hills. The American Civil War, by cutting down upon the normal imports of foodstuffs from the United States, served to aggravate the general situation.

The planters were bitter, and directed much of their hostility towards the Baptist and other non-conforming missionaries who had been the Negro's chief support. It was understandable that the non-conformist missionaries should identify themselves with the Negro, for while they had no hope of converting Anglican planters, the Negro was ripe for redemption from sin and paganism. During the years of slavery, only these missionaries had worked conscientiously to improve his status and to educate him. Many thousands of blacks had been baptized, although even these showed an undimmed reverence for the con-jurors of black magic, the shamanistic Obeah men. Con-versions continued after emancipation. According to the census of 1861, Jamaica counted a population of 440,000 people, 13,000 of them white. Of this number, some 130,000 attended a church. The sect with the most nu-merous adherents were the Wesleyans, the most conserva-tive of the dissenting groups, followed closely by the es-tablished Church of England. The heart of doctrinal and political dissent was to be found among the over 26,000 Jamaica Baptists. In 1831, Baptist missionaries had even been strongly implicated in a slave revolt.

Jamaica had an 'advanced' constitution, granted by Charles II in 1662, and similar to those which had been issued to many of the thirteen mainland colonies at about the same time. While in some crown colonies, the Governor acted independently of legislative control, and in others he was assisted by an appointed council, in Jamaica, the Governor was flanked by both a council and an elective assembly of 47 members. The voting of supplies, of the appropriations bill, rested entirely with the Assembly. Though, technically, Jamaica had 'representative' government, it was far from democratic. The election law in force during Governor Eyre's tenure—that of 1858—had given the vote only to those who met certain property qualifications. During the election of 1864, only 1,903 Jamaicans were qualified to vote for members of the Assembly. The property qualifications for those who wished to hold a seat in the assembly were even higher. In the century preceding 1865, there had been three serious insurrections—in 1760, in 1795, and in 1831, during which times there had been wild talk among the Negroes of massacring the whites. After 'emancipation,' Negro extremists, pointing to the fact that over 400,000 Negroes were under the legislative control of a 47-man planter oligarchy chosen by fewer than 2,000 electors, continued to pose the solution of revolt and massacre.

For over two years, Eyre was to remain in Jamaica as Acting Governor, being repeatedly informed that he was soon to be replaced. Of course, such a tenuous hold made for difficulties, but certain features of Eyre's character increased these difficulties immeasurably. Almost immediately upon coming to Jamaica, he became involved in what has become known as the Tramway Scandal. In his anxiety to get a tramway constructed with the utmost speed, Eyre had violated several local laws and had become a party, however unwitting, to an attempt to defraud the Jamaican Government. His intentions had been honourable—there was no question at all of lining his own pockets—he had simply been gulled by people whose motives were less pure, in this case an embezzling colonial engineer. In the fashion of weak men, once he had determined upon a course of action, Eyre refused to be moved by all the evidence in the world. Inevitably, the

Governor's stubbornness aroused the irritation of members of his executive committee, of the Jamaican press, of the House of Assembly. The assembly finally refused to pass the annual Money Bill until Eyre had rid himself of certain advisers, including the engineer and a certain Baron von Ketelhodt, a German who had married an Englishwoman with Jamaican property and who had become a special favourite of the Governor. Eyre responded by dissolving the Jamaica Assembly, and informing the Colonial office in London that he had done so because of the Assembly's refusal to pass the Money Bill, making no mention of the Tramway incident. In England, Eyre was regarded as unimpeachable, and an attempt by the Assembly to present its side was answered by a sharp reprimand from the Colonial Secretary.

After having thus received the support of the Colonial Office, Eyre was more determined to have his way. He would brook no interference; the tramway would be built. He refused even to *listen* to the arguments of opponents, one of whom, George Price, was a member of his executive committee. Price insisted that the Governor go carefully over the fraudulent estimates, and even had a piece of the track already laid shipped to the Colonial Office for examination. Although the London experts replied that it was below usable standards, Eyre refused to be swayed. Finally Price demanded that the Governor either prosecute the corrupt Colonial Engineer, who had stood to profit considerably by the building of the tramway, or Price threatened to write to the Duke of Newcastle relating the details of the whole business. Still reluctant, Eyre became hesitant, for the Governor was always careful about making the most favourable impression upon his superiors, and was worried about how they might react to Price's story. Finally, Eyre agreed to examine the estimates, and to see the track already laid. Gradually he became convinced that fraud had indeed been intended. Still anxious about his standing with the Colonial Office, Eyre attempted a compromise with Price. He agreed to prosecute the Colonial Engineer, however not about the tramway fraud, but about another bit of recently uncovered corruption in

which Eyre himself had not been involved. Price stood his
ground and insisted that the Engineer be prosecuted for
his part in the tramway question. Eyre most reluctantly
agreed to these terms just in time to prevent Price from
dispatching his letter on the London boat.

The tramway incident should have served as a lesson
for the new Governor, but in his subsequent relations with
his Executive Committee and with the Assembly, Eyre
continued his high-handed behaviour, continued to disregard island laws and showed an unblushing desire to de-
ceive the Colonial Office about island conditions. There
were further conflicts with the Assembly, and in the spring
of 1864, that body began to take steps to secure Eyre's
recall by the Colonial Office. Sir Frederic Rogers, the
Permanent Under-Secretary for the Colonies, defended
Eyre against this criticism and even persuaded the Duke
of Newcastle to make Eyre's temporary appointment a
permanent one. The Duke died before he could act, but
his successor in office, Edward Cardwell, on Rogers' advice, informed Eyre, much to the latter's surprise, that his
appointment had been made permanent. The Jamaica Assembly was immensely disappointed.

Eyre's reputation had slipped badly by early 1864.
Known to be puritanical, he was poorly thought of by the
easy-going planters who loved their rum and mulatto mis-
tresses, and, furthermore, his refusal to entertain lavishly
as had been customary among his predecessors, gave him
the character of meanness. Eyre was a thoroughgoing
Anglican and hated Dissenters, Methodists and Baptists,
who formed a majority of the island's inhabitants, and
they, needless to add, returned his distaste. Eyre could
perhaps serve as a 'protector' of the backward and sub-
missive Australian 'blackfellow,' who permitted such con-
descension, but Jamaican freedmen, aspiring to privileges
of equality, roused his anger. So neither among planters
nor populace had he been able to obtain support. In early
1864, the *Jamaica Guardian* had written:

Governor Eyre is daily becoming more unpopular, and
nothing could give greater satisfaction to persons of all

classes in the country than to hear that he has been recalled. People long for a change. His Excellency will not do. Weak, vacillating, and undignified in his conduct and character, he has lost caste exceedingly.

The *Morning Journal,* the organ of the planters' party, wrote in much the same spirit:

The newspapers received by the packet make no mention whatever of the recall of Mr Eyre from the administration of the affairs of this Colony, an event to which the Colonists had been looking forward with intense anxiety. His Excellency has worn out the patience and forbearance of every person here. The Editor of the *Guardian* has publicly announced his intention of memorializing the Colonial Secretary against the highhanded proceedings of His Excellency; and we expect it will not be long before similar memorials will be transmitted to Downing Street from the people of the twenty-two parishes. . . . The feebleness of his understanding makes him unfit to represent the Majesty of the Crown—to conduct the grave business of state. His capacity is scarcely equal to what his great place requires. . . .

The Colonial Office, however, refused to listen to the steadily accumulating evidence against its governor. Sir Frederick Rogers, especially, had a stake in defending the wisdom of the appointment, made upon his recommendation, and his subsequent positions in support of Eyre.

The uprising of October 1865 which was to break out in the parish of St Thomas-in-the-East involved one of the landowners of that district, George William Gordon. Gordon, the illegitimate son of a wealthy white Jamaican planter and a Negro slave woman, was a man of ability, who had taught himself to read, to write, and to calculate, and had been able to obtain his own freedom as well as that of his mother. He began a career as a produce merchant, and had been sufficiently successful to secure the freedom of his slave sisters, as well, and even to send them to school in Europe. In the years following, Gordon's white father made unwise speculations and finally found himself on the verge of bankruptcy. The planter's ex-slave son, in story-book fashion, saved his father's estate, and even contributed to the support of his legitimate white half-brothers and sisters, although they refused even to nod to him on the street. Gordon married a white girl, whose mother kept a girls' school at Kingston and, from report, showed himself as generous to his wife's family as to his own. By the 'sixties, Gordon had become a landowner and planter, grown wealthy enough to be made a magistrate in St Thomas' parish. A religious man, reared as a member of the United Presbyterian Church of Scotland, he had become a Baptist, and a Baptist lay preacher, thereby sharing in the eyes of Eyre and of the planters the opprobrium associated with that sect. Though he would have been welcomed as a member of the dominant, planter group—as other coloured men had been— his sympathies were with the blacks, and he kept an isolated position.

There were two principal parties in the Jamaica legislature, the Town party and the Country party. The Country party was the party of the white planters. The Town party was largely composed of people of colour, descendants of white fathers and slave concubines, who either had been manumitted or had managed to purchase their freedom, and were now officials, of various sorts, merchants, and lawyers, although there were also some planters in their number. Much of the press, with coloured proprietors, generally supported the Town party. For some decades before the arrival of Eyre, Governors of Jamaica had found in the Town party a valuable ally in their fights with the planter aristocracy, which the middle-class townsmen sought to displace as the governing group. Yet Governor Eyre had, quite early in his stay in Jamaica, identified himself with the planters, and had thereby incurred the enmity of the Town party—and, most particularly, of the leader of the small left-wing of that party, Gordon. By 1865, however, Governor Eyre, perhaps because he was becoming alarmed by the intransigent hostility of Gordon and his 'demagogues,' had decided to make his peace with the Town party, and had indicated that he now meant to support its claim to share power with the planters. The leadership of the party became more kindly disposed towards Eyre, but Gordon—who, supported by his little band of 'demagogues,' served as the spokesman for the settlers in the hill country and the impoverished blacks in the towns or still on the sugar estates—remained a bitter enemy.

Gordon had long been an active reformer, and his efforts to improve the conditions of Jamaica's poor Negroes secured for him the hatred of the island's governing class who saw in him the instigator of all troubles. His every attempt at action brought him difficulties. For example, in his position as a magistrate, he had tried to clean up a disgracefully unsanitary jail at Morant Bay, to establish it upon efficient operating principles. In 1862, shortly after Eyre had arrived in Jamaica, Magistrate Gordon had written to the Governor about conditions in the jail and made other suggestions about the administration of justice in the parish. The white planters of the district were angry at this interference. Their leader, the Governor's new friend Baron von Ketelhodt, easily persuaded Eyre to remove Gordon from his position as magistrate. Exasperated by the failure of the Governor to even listen to his side of the story, Gordon appealed to the Colonial Office. In a private communication to the Governor, who had after all just arrived on the island, the Colonial Office informed him that Gordon had indeed been within his rights and that Eyre had gone far beyond his own powers. Publicly, however, the Office backed the action of its Governor in suspending Gordon. To Gordon, all this could only appear as outrageous injustice. He determined to run for election to the House of Assembly, and when his opportunity came in the election of March 1863, he ran and won.

In the Assembly, he presented further difficulties for the Governor and the planters' party. Time and again, Gordon attacked the undertakings of the Governor and impugned his intelligence, a course which did not endear him to Eyre who began to think of him as his chief personal antagonist and the leading trouble-maker on the island. Gordon was reckless and violent in his Assembly speeches. He clearly thought of himself as fighting single-handedly the battle for God and Truth against the forces of the Devil, and, inevitably, exaggerated his case. After the events at Morant Bay, Eyre's defenders quoted one of his more hot-headed speeches—delivered some months before the uprising—to prove that Gordon had long been plotting insurrection. In the midst of an address to the Assembly, in which he called Eyre 'grovelling, pretentious, and prevaricating,' and opined that 'it does not seem that His Excellency's natural endowments qualify him for the government of this country,' the Speaker called Gordon to order, demanded he stop employing such insulting terms. Whereupon Gordon protested at the Speaker's attempt to

suppress public opinion, to pen up the expression of public indignation; but I tell you that it will soon burst forth like a flood, and sweep everything before it. There must be a limit to everything: a limit to oppression—a limit to transgression—and a limit to illegality! These proceedings remind me of the time of Herod. . . .

I do not think that any Governor has ever acted so before. While he justifies himself in one case, he uses the police force to accomplish another illegality. What an example to the prisoners who were confined in prison! What an example to the people! If the Governor is to go on in this way, what can you expect from the populace?

Another Member:—Insurrection. (Laughter)

Mr Gordon:—Ah! that will be the result. When all over laws are put at defiance, the populace will break out from discontent, and the Governor will be unable to allay their feelings. . . . When a Governor becomes a dictator, when he becomes despotic, it is time for the people to dethrone him. . . . I have never seen an animal more voracious for cruelty and power than the present Governor of Jamaica.

Mr Speaker:—Order! Order! Such language cannot be allowed. . . .

Mr Gordon:—I say that if the law is to be disregarded it will lead to anarchy and bloodshed. . . . If we are to be governed by such a Governor much longer, the people will have to fly to arms and become self-governing.

There were shouts of protest, cries for order, and after the disturbance had subsided, one of Eyre's supporters called Gordon 'a disgrace to the House.'

Of course, as most members of the Assembly understood, this talk was largely rhetoric. We belong to a generation which has become more accustomed to such violent words from colonial leaders—displays of oratory rather than intention. The bulk of the evidence would indicate that Gordon considered himself a loyal servant of the Queen and that the fomenting of insurrection was far from his mind. But his words may have had a different meaning to the embittered blacks who had come to regard him as their spokesman, and were inclined to take his speeches at face value.

Since Gordon had openly declared himself the enemy of both the Governor and of the rich planters, it was natural that they should harass him in turn. On 10th May 1865, Gordon wrote a letter to Louis Chamerovzow, the Secretary of the British Anti-Slavery Society, widely known through the Empire as the defender of the emancipated blacks:

I have to contend with hatred and persecution of no ordinary kind at present. You will, by a paper sent you herewith, see that the Governor, the Judge (of the Circuit Court), the Attorney-General and a special jury, are all conspiring against me here: and I believe that if some of them found the opportunity, they would unscrupulously dispatch me.

In 1859, Edward Bean Underhill had visited the island
of Jamaica and had made a study of conditions there. Dr
Underhill was the Joint Secretary of the Baptist Missionary
Society and, after his return to England, he continued to
keep in touch with Jamaican affairs through correspondence with Baptist ministers on the island. The news of
increasing economic distress which he had received
throughout 1864 had disturbed him greatly and, in January of 1865, he wrote a lengthy letter to the Secretary
of State for the Colonies, Edward Cardwell, reporting the
unhappy circumstances of the coloured population. To
improve conditions, Underhill proposed that the Crown
promote the formation of producers' cooperatives among
the black freeholders in order to enable them to profitably
raise such exportable crops as spices, tobacco, coffee and
cotton since sugar-growing had proved so hazardous, and
suggested that Jamaica's tax system be overhauled to encourage greater capital investment on the island. This
analysis of the island's economy showed an understanding
rare for the time, and it was many years before the Colonial Office was to see the situation in the same light.
Underhill concluded his letter with a protest against the
Jamaica Assembly's 'unjust taxation of the coloured population,' its 'refusal of just tribunals,' and its 'denial of political rights to the emancipated negroes.'

Cardwell forwarded Underhill's letter to Governor Eyre
for reply. The Governor grew violently angry upon reading the 'baptist charges,' sent copies to the leading planters
and other island dignitaries, and asked them to report on
conditions in their own parishes. The Governor's corre-
spondents replied either that distress did not exist or, if
they admitted economic trouble, attributed it to Negro
laziness. (As we have indicated, there is no doubt that
many Negroes squatted upon unoccupied land rather than
work for the planters at poor wages. The white planters
did everything possible to prevent this: for example, in
order to keep the blacks from taking full advantage of the
bread-fruit, coconuts and other slow-growing trees which
they had planted, whole Negro villages were, periodically,

forcibly moved.) Eyre then published the Underhill letter along with the replies he had stimulated and had them widely distributed. In a dispatch to Cardwell, Eyre summed up the 'evidence' received, reporting that not the black labourer but the planter had suffered more because of recent adverse economic conditions, that, in fact, the position of the Jamaican black was far superior to that of the peasantry of most European countries. The cause of Jamaican depression was the laziness and untrustworthiness of the black, a failure in moral fibre which produced poverty and crime on the island, etc., etc.

Negro leaders on the island perceived that Underhill had understood their difficulties, and rejoiced in finding a champion in London. Throughout Jamaica, mass meetings—'Underhill meetings'—were held to support his views. Resolutions were carefully framed, read to the assemblage, adopted by acclamation, all in most orderly manner. In some instances, petitions were drafted to be sent to the Queen. To Eyre such lawful meetings seemed the height of sedition, much as similar meetings in Central Africa were to appear to resident Colonial officials, almost a century later. In Eyre's mind, the whole country was on the brink of bloody revolution, and had been brought to that state by Underhill. Early in 1865, a petition drafted by an Underhill meeting was sent to Eyre for forwarding to Her Majesty, Queen Victoria. The petition, signed by the 'poor people' of St Ann's Parish, told the Queen of the poverty of her loyal Jamaican subjects and humbly requested Victoria to rent them, for cultivation, the unused royal lands. In forwarding the petition, as was his duty, Eyre appended this note:

This is the first fruits of Dr Underhill's letter, which represented the peasantry of Jamaica as being generally in a destitute, starving, and naked condition . . . and I fear the result of Dr Underhill's communication and the circulars of the Baptist Missionary Society will have a very prejudicial influence in unsettling the minds of the peasantry.

Eyre's view was seconded by the Colonial Office which drafted the 'Queen's reply':

> THE PROSPERITY of the labouring classes, as well as of all other classes, depends in Jamaica, and in other communities, upon their working for wages, not uncertainly, or capriciously, but steadily and continuously, at the times when their labour is wanted, and for so long as it is wanted; AND THAT if they would use this industry, and thereby render the plantations productive, they would enable the planters to pay them higher wages for the same hours of work than are received by the best field labourers in this country; and, as the cost of the necessaries of life is much less in Jamaica than it is here, they would be enabled, by adding prudence to industry, to lay by an ample provision for seasons of drought and dearth; AND THEY may be assured, that it is from their own industry and prudence, in availing themselves of the means of prospering that are before them, and not from any such schemes as have been suggested to them, that they must look for an improvement in their conditions.

The Queen's letter—a masterpiece of Victorian economic prejudice—was irrelevant. The great majority of Jamaicans did not depend upon wages for their income, but worked upon their own land or upon rented land. Furthermore, the presumption that there *were* jobs available was untrue. Many of the leaders of the Jamaican blacks were loyally convinced that the Queen could never have written such a callous letter. They preferred to believe that the Governor had never forwarded the petition and had himself constructed the reply. One passage which especially disturbed Jamaica's freedmen, was that which spoke of steady and continuous employment. This led many of the back-country blacks to presume that Eyre intended to re-introduce slavery on the island, for the core of what the emancipated Negro understood by freedom was the right to give or withhold labour as he pleased. Signing a labour contract for continuous work seemed too much like the days before emancipation.

After the posting of the Queen's reply, speeches at the Underhill meetings became more inflammatory. At the end of July, a printed manifesto was distributed to the people of the neighbouring parishes of St Thomas' and St Ann's, the purpose of which was to collect a good crowd for a public meeting scheduled to be held at the Court House at Morant Bay on July 29th. The eloquently phrased appeal was supposed to have been written by George William Gordon:

> We know that our beloved Queen is too noble-hearted to say anything unkind even to her most humble subjects. . . . People of St Ann's . . . you have no sugar estates to work on nor can find other employment. We call on you to come forth. Even if you be naked come forth and protest against the unjust representations made against you by Mr Governor Eyre and his band of Custodes. . . .

> People of St Thomas-in-the-East, you have been ground down too long already. Shake off your sloth. . . . The Government have dared you to defend your rights against the enormities of an unscrupulous and oppressive foreigner, Mr Custos Ketelhodt. . . . The Custos, we learn, read at the last vestry the despatch from Mr Cardwell, which he seemed to think should quiet you; but how can men with a sense of wrong in their bosoms be content to be quiet with such a reproachful despatch as this?

> Remember that he only is free whom the truth makes free. You are no longer slaves but free men. . . .

The scheduled meeting did not take place until August 12th. The Custos of the parish, Baron von Ketelhodt, had refused permission to use the Court House, so the meeting was held in the open air. A deputation—including a local firebrand, Paul Bogle, a landowner and a Baptist Negro leader, and a sometime business associate of Gordon—was selected by the meeting to present the parish's complaints to the Governor at Spanish Town. When the deputation arrived at the Governor's door, it was told that Eyre would not see them. The delegates returned home in ugly humour. This was particularly true of Bogle, who in August and September, spoke often in St Thomas' parish. With mounting fury, he denounced the Governor, the Custos, the Queen and soon, every white man. His efforts to promote racial hatred among his listeners, though, proved largely unsuccessful.

From this time on, there was a split among the Negroes of St Thomas' parish. George William Gordon headed the moderate party which was supported by the bulk of the parish, and began to collect subscriptions of money to be used to send a deputation to London which would present a petition to the Queen, personally, thus circumventing Governor Eyre. Paul Bogle, on the other hand, was organizing small, secret societies whose long-range purpose was to foment rebellion and drive the white man from Jamaica. Reports of illegal drillings, of the collection of small arms and ammunition, and of clandestine meetings poured in upon Kingston. Trouble was reported in parishes throughout the island. In some regions, Negroes had refused to pay taxes.

Trouble actually began at the town of Morant Bay in St Thomas' parish on 7th October 1865. It was a Saturday and a market day, and a Court of Petty Sessions was being held. The business before the court was of a routine nature—mostly cases of assault, both physical assault and assault growing out of the use of abusive language, and all the cases involved Negroes. In one, a woman plaintiff charged that she had been assaulted by a boy. The case was heard and the boy, found guilty, was fined four shillings as well as the costs of the trial, some 12s 6d. A Negro named Geoghegan rose in the courtroom and told the boy to pay the fine only, not the costs. There was a commotion in the court. The magistrates ordered the constables on duty to seize Geoghegan, who was loudly shouting his advice, but the constables soon found that they were being opposed by by-standers who succeeded in rescuing Geoghegan from the courthouse. When the constables tried to follow, they were beaten back. It was this incident which was later regarded as 'the first resistance to lawful authority' at Morant Bay.

The court had been crowded on that particular Saturday because of the wide interest taken in a land case which was to be heard—and Paul Bogle was reported to have been present and to have been one of those who had helped effect Geoghegan's rescue. On the Monday following, on October 9th, warrants were issued for the arrest of Bogle and several others who had been involved in Saturday's riot. On Tuesday morning, six policemen and two constables, all of them Negroes, set off for Stony Gut, the Negro village, about five miles from Morant Bay, where Bogle lived. Bogle was in his yard when they arrived. The police informed him that they had a warrant for his arrest, and Bogle asked them to read it. After the reading, one of the policemen started to seize hold of him, and Bogle, according to a police report, shouted 'Help, here.' From the bushes came another shout of 'Turn out, men,' and almost immediately between 300 and 500 men armed with cutlasses, sticks, and spikes rushed out of the Baptist chapel in which Bogle was a regular preacher. They attacked the policemen and quickly overpowered them. Three policemen were taken prisoner and later released after being compelled to take an oath that, in the future, they would 'join their colour,' and 'cleave to the black.' They returned to Morant Bay bringing to Custos von Ketelhodt, Bogle's threat to come with his men to the Bay on the following day.

When von Ketelhodt heard this, he ordered the Volunteers, a citizen reserve force, to assemble and to guard the Court House, and wrote Governor Eyre for help:

> I deeply regret that it is my duty to bring to the notice of His Excellency the Governor, that a serious outbreak among certain of the labouring population in

this neighbourhood is threatened, and in fact has already commenced. . . .

I cannot hesitate under these circumstances, to submit that it is very probable that without some military aid, the force at the disposal of the authorities will, in the event of the people carrying out their threats, be insufficient to uphold the law, and, in that case, the worst consequences must be anticipated.

Eyre received von Ketelhodt's letter on Wednesday, the morning after its dispatch, and sprang into action. For some months now, the leaders of the planters had been warning Eyre to expect violence. Extremists among the Negroes, Eyre had been informed, had even spoken of making Jamaica an independent republic like Haiti, talk which terrified those who remembered the slaughter of Frenchmen by Haitian 'republicans.' Eyre called together a meeting of the Executive Council and, after hurried consultation, arranged to send 100 men aboard Her Majesty's ship *Wolverine* to Morant Bay.

Feeling that, for the moment, all was well in hand, Eyre returned to his home in the mountains near Spanish Town to attend a dinner party, a festive occasion at which the Governor seemed unworried. On the following afternoon, a Thursday, Eyre received another report from Morant Bay. 'The blacks have risen,' was the chilling message, and the report went on to tell how the Negroes had murdered the Governor's friend, Baron von Ketelhodt, as well as two sons of the rector of St Thomas' parish, and how the volunteers had valiantly but unsuccessfully tried to defend the courthouse from Paul Bogle's men. The rebellious blacks, the report continued, were now proceeding westward, destroying property and murdering whites along their line of march. Another hundred troops were immediately dispatched by ship to Morant Bay, and a company of troops left Kingston to intercept the rebels marching westward. A little before midnight, a meeting of the Privy Council, summoned by the Governor, solemnly declared that it would be expedient to proclaim martial law and the following morning such a proclamation was issued for the entire county of Surrey, excepting only the city of Kingston. Later that same day, Friday the 13th of October, Governor Eyre set sail for Morant Bay with a detachment of fifty additional troops. Eyre was accompanied by the adjutant to the commanding general, a Colonel Nelson, whom the Governor made a Brigadier-General for the occasion, and to whom he entrusted the command of all troops at Morant Bay.

On its way, the Governor's ship met the returning *Wolverine*, bringing white 'refugees' from the fighting. The *Wolverine* stopped so that a letter to Eyre from the Clerk of the Peace of St Thomas' might be delivered. The letter described the events of the battle of the court house in frightening terms:

About three o'clock in the evening, and while the vestry was still sitting, a band of music was heard, and shortly after, from about 400 to 500 men appeared, armed with sticks, cutlasses, spears, guns, and other deadly weapons. The Custos then appeared on the steps of the Court-house, and entreated the people not to come into the square of the Court-house, and requested to know of what they complained. At this time the volunteers, eighteen in number, were drawn up in front of the Court-house; the mob still persisted in entering the square, and when about fifty yards from the volunteers the Riot Act was read by the Custos, but which had no effect on the rioters. On the rioters coming within ten yards of the volunteers they fired a volley of stones at them; the order was then given to fire, and several of the rioters killed. The fury of the rioters was such that everyone had to take refuge inside the Court-house; several shots were fired into the Court-house, the windows were all smashed to pieces, and ultimately fired and burnt down; his Honour the Custos was murdered in the most brutal and savage manner, with other magistrates and gentlemen of the parish.

Eyre questioned the refugees on board the *Wolverine*. He found their stories 'shocking' and 'harrowing' (these were the words he was to use in the report on the uprising sent a week later to the Colonial Secretary). 'The most fearful atrocities were perpetrated,' the Governor's report was to relate.

The Island curate of Bath, the Rev. V. Herschell, is said to have had his tongue cut out whilst still alive, and an attempt is said to have been made to skin him. One person (Mr Charles Price, a black gentleman, formerly a Member of the Assembly) was ripped open, and his entrails taken out. One gentleman (Lieutenant Hall of the Volunteers) is said to have been pushed into an outbuilding, which was then set on fire, and kept there until he was literally roasted alive. Many are said to have had their eyes scooped out; heads were cleft open and the brains taken out. The Baron's fingers were cut off and carried away as trophies by the murderers. Some bodies were half-burnt, others horribly battered. Indeed the whole outrage could only be paralleled by the atrocities of the Indian mutiny. The women, as usual on such occasions, were even more brutal and barbarous than the men. The only redeeming trait being that, so far as we could learn, no ladies or children had as yet been injured.

It is easy to imagine the mood of Eyre and his soldiers after hearing these stories. When they arrived at the Bay, small bodies of troops were immediately dispatched inland on 'reconnoitering' missions. Every effort was made to find 'rebels' who seemed, somehow, to have disappeared. A small party of troops surprised some 'rebels' in their huts at about two o'clock in the morning. They captured two men and some women. The elder of the men was tried by court martial and hanged. The second, a youngster in his earliest teens, was simply flogged. On October 14th, five more prisoners were tried by court martial and four of these were hanged on the stone archway of the courthouse which the blacks had burned three days before. The remaining prisoner was flogged. Other reconnoitering parties had similar results. Rebels—a 'rebel' was any Negro who had not fled before the troops came—were hanged or flogged. No organized opposition of any sort was encountered, however. By Sunday, October 15th, Eyre reported that 'all our most important work' being done, the troops were enabled to rest in their barracks. For all purposes then, the 'insurrection' at Morant Bay had been suppressed, or so Eyre's dispatch would have led anyone to believe. But the following morning, after the end of the Sabbath day, began the work of retribution. A court martial sat to try newly captured prisoners and twenty-seven were found guilty and hanged.

Eyre was satisfied with the proceedings. Convinced that the suppression of the rebellion was in the good hands of General Nelson, the Governor set off in the *Wolverine* for Kingston, arriving at the capital early Tuesday morning. He found Kingston in terror because of the reports of the Morant Bay white 'refugees.' There was much talk of Jamaica becoming another Haiti. An American trader who had on hand a large stock of faulty pistols sailed for Kingston as soon as he heard of the rebellion. Because of the panic, he was able to dispose of his entire stock at fabulous prices. When his last pistol was sold, he left hastily though not without remarking to a Kingston friend that the only people who could be hurt by his badly damaged revolvers were those who tried to use them.

Eyre's return to the capital with the news that matters at the Bay were well in hand moderated some fears, but there was still uneasiness. At Kingston, Eyre received a report from the commander of the land forces trying to intercept the rebel bands marching westward. The commander, Colonel Hobbs, wrote that he was moving on the rebel stronghold at Stony Gut, but had thus far not encountered any organized resistance. But he had not idled along his line of march—he had shot at every black man he saw. In this, Hobbs was acting in accordance with orders he had received from the Deputy Adjutant General, Colonel Elkington. In a letter to the commander in the field, Elkington had written:

Dear Colonel,

    I send you an order to push on at once to Stony Gut, but I trust you are there already. Hole is doing splendid service all about Manchioneal, and shooting every black man who cannot account for himself (sixty on line of march). Nelson at Port Antonio hanging like fun by court martial. I hope you will not send any black prisoners. Do punish the blackguards well.

In early November a Jamaican newspaper correspondent reported that the water of the Morant Bay River had become unwholesome because of the number of dead bodies lying in it. 'It was in this district,' he wrote, 'that the 6th, under Colonel Hobbs, marched in their way from Monklands to Stoney Gut, and no doubt they dealt out the flying rebels their righteous desert.'

The Governor had returned to Kingston to complete an important piece of business. As he was later to report to the Colonial Secretary, he had found, during the past several days, 'the most unmistakable evidence that Mr Geo. W. Gordon, a coloured Member of the House of Assembly, had not only been mixed up in the matter, but was himself, through his own misrepresentation and seditious language addressed to the ignorant black people the chief cause and origin of the whole rebellion.' Gordon was in Kingston at this time, and Eyre swore out a warrant for his arrest. Though ill, Gordon voluntarily surrendered himself as soon as he heard of the warrant. Kingston was not under martial law—the ordinary civil courts were still functioning. Should Gordon be left to his trial—the charge of having conspired to instigate the revolt—by the civil courts of Kingston? Governor Eyre decided against this course, and personally hustled him on board the *Wolverine* and set sail for Morant Bay where military courts were in session.

    Why had Eyre acted so high-handedly? Eyre's enemies were to contend that the Governor knew—given the absence of any real evidence connecting Gordon with the insurrection—that the Kingston courts would be forced to

set him free. Eyre's defenders, on the other hand, asserted
that Gordon's court martial was necessary to the effective
suppression of the insurrection. Eyre himself declared, in
his report to the Colonial Secretary, that 'considering it
right in the abstract, and desirable as a matter of policy,
that whilst the poor black men who had been misled were
undergoing condign punishment, the chief instigator of all
the evils should not go unpunished.'

On the 18th of October, the *Wolverine*, with Eyre and
Gordon aboard, entered Morant Bay. After disembarking,
Eyre escorted Gordon to the military headquarters and
placed him in the hands of General Nelson. Then the
Governor returned to the *Wolverine* and set sail for Kingston. Preparations were immediately set afoot at Morant
Bay to court martial the mulatto member of the House
of Assembly. The court martial was a farce: a young and
inexperienced naval lieutenant, Herbert Brand, was asked
by Nelson to preside over the trial; there was no Judge
Advocate General to advise on points of law; the evidence
presented would have been thought insufficient even for
an indictment in a civil court, no less a conviction. Again
and again, Gordon was prevented from saying anything
in his own defence. On Saturday, October 21st, the court
martial found Gordon guilty of having conspired to foment
insurrection and sentenced him to be hanged by the neck.
Since the following day was a Sunday and the Sabbath,
the execution of sentence was delayed until Monday, the
23rd of October. In the interim, General Nelson whose
job it was to confirm the proceedings, had become disturbed. It was one thing to hang ignorant blacks, men
without property and standing, but quite another to exe-
cute a wealthy property-owner and a member of the Assembly. He delayed confirming the sentence until Eyre
could be consulted in Kingston. Eyre was consulted and,
before the time set for Gordon's hanging on Monday, the
Governor had written Nelson that he fully approved. Nelson speedily confirmed sentence and the preparations for
the execution proceeded.

Feeling against Gordon was high among the planters

during these days of trouble. They shared Eyre's view of Gordon's ultimate responsibility for provoking the insurrection and the Governor's determination that the mulatto be executed. This attitude was reflected in the description of his death written by an eye-witness, a reporter for the *Colonial Standard*: 'There he stood high above all the other rebels, beneath the great arch of the burnt Court House, with his hands and feet pinioned, and the halter already around his neck,' the reporter wrote. 'Beneath him were the steps on which he was wont to stand when haranguing a multitude on the days of election. Through the same archway, more than once, have an infuriated mob rushed into the sanctum of the Queen's hall of justice, inflamed with passions roused by this deluded man's teachings, and it seemed the hand of retributive justice that doomed him to meet his death on the very spot of his vile machinations.'

Eyre devoted the last part of his report to the Colonial Secretary to an analysis of the outbreak. He had yet to find a 'reasonable or intelligible cause' of the 'origin of this most wicked and widespread rebellion,' but he could not himself 'doubt that it is in a great degree due to Dr Underhill's letter and the meetings held in connexion with that letter.' At these meetings, 'language of the most exciting and seditious kind was constantly used, and the people told plainly to right themselves, to be up and doing, to put their shoulders to the wheel, to do as the Haitians had done, and other similar advice.'

> The parties who have more immediately taken part in these nefarious proceedings [the Governor's report continued] are: firstly, G. W. Gordon, a member of Assembly and a Baptist preacher; secondly, several black persons, chiefly of the Baptist persuasion, connected with him; [and] a few Baptist missionaries, who . . . endorse at public meetings or otherwise, all the untruthly statements or innuendoes propagated in Dr Underhill's letter. . . .

Eyre asserted that 'the promptitude and vigour of action which has at once grappled with and punished the rebellion, has been the saving of Jamaica.' 'The whole colony,' Eyre continued, 'has been upon a mine, which required but a spark to ignite it.' If he had not acted swiftly, Eyre maintained, the insurrection would have spread over the entire island since 'disaffection and disloyalty still exist in nearly all the parishes.' If that had happened, 'either the Colony would have been lost to the mother country, or an almost interminable war and an unknown expense have had to be incurred in suppressing it.' 'I trust, Sir,' Eyre concluded, 'that you will fully bear these circumstances in mind, and that, in doing so, you will not regard the just severity which has been exercised otherwise than as a merciful substitute for the much larger measure of punishment which would have had to be executed had the rebellion been allowed time to gather head and extend itself.' Eyre took upon himself 'the whole responsibility of what has been done,' although he bestowed praise upon the conduct of Lieutenant Brand, upon General Nelson, and upon Colonel Hobbs.

It was not until the 16th of November that the mail packet bearing Governor Eyre's report arrived at London. The Governor's report had been anxiously awaited, since the news of insurrection had become known through the gossip of passengers on a previous packet, and from bundles of Jamaican newspapers. The press had reprinted those stories for the eager consumption of a news-hungry public. The Governor's report was devoured with no less eagerness by the Colonial Office. Devoured but not scrutinized, or there might have been some uneasy questions. For example, despite Eyre's repetition of stories of rebel armies, at no time did the troops in the field meet any organized opposition, although the reconnoitering companies were small in number—between twenty-five and fifty men—and the rebels were reputed to be in the hundreds and even thousands, and heavily armed. Furthermore, there had not been a single British military casualty, although, as Eyre reported, the troops had 'suffered much inconvenience and hardship from the state of the weather which has been extremely wet and inclement.' This circumstance should have been immediately noted by the officials in London, for was there not something incongruous in a revolution which endangers an entire island but is yet invisible to troops in the field? Then, too, the dubious legality of the Gordon affair went, for the moment, unnoticed. The chief reaction of the Colonial Office was relief that the worst seemed over, that order had been restored, and that the British flag still flew over the Governor's mansion at Spanish Town.

The day after the receipt of Eyre's report, the Secretary of State for the Colonies, Edward Cardwell, wrote to the Governor of Jamaica to congratulate him on his 'spirit, energy, and judgment.' 'It was the first duty of your Government to take, as you did, effectual measures for the suppression of this horrible rebellion, and I congratulate you on the rapid success by which these measures appear to have been attended,' Cardwell wrote. Eyre had appended to his dispatch some military reports from commanders in the field. Cardwell apologized for not having had the time to examine them thoroughly, but in his brief perusal he had noted that there were some matters which required clarification. However, that could await a time when Eyre had greater leisure. In the meanwhile, Cardwell assured the Governor, he was willing to put his full trust in Eyre's character and in that of his officers. Cardwell did not in the slightest doubt that 'it will appear that you have arrested the course of punishment as soon as you were able to do so, and have exerted yourself to confine it meanwhile to ascertained offenders and to cases of aggravated guilt.'

In the weeks that followed, the Colonial Office was to regret these hasty congratulations. Mass meetings of protest and delegations from Exeter Hall societies, and the bludgeonings of the Radical press caused Cardwell to accede to demands for a Commission of Inquiry. For some months, controversy over the events in Jamaica was muted, as the public awaited the report of the Inquiry Commission.

One important result of the Morant Bay uprising—a demonstration of disgust at the government's refusal to understand the aspirations of the black settlers in the hills—was the end of Jamaican self-government. On 7th November 1865, in a speech to the Jamaican legislature, Eyre, citing the recent uprising as evidence, warned of the growing threat that the blacks would win the suffrage and control the island. He, then, easily persuaded both parties in the Assembly to abolish that body and to petition London to make Jamaica a Crown Colony.

3

THE JAMAICA COMMITTEE AND
PARLIAMENT:
J. S. MILL

The events in Jamaica occurred at a strategic time in English political life. Consequently, instead of merely forming the material for sermons in dissenting chapels, they became the subject for parliamentary debates. Indignation over the Jamaica events did not remain the exclusive property of dignified delegations to the colonial secretary, it belonged as well to great working-class mass meetings. It was not relegated to the tea-table conversations of the Mrs Jellybys of the day, but became the occasion for the entrance upon the public stage of the most honoured names in Victorian letters and science.

On 18th October 1865, three days after the insurrection had begun some thousands of miles away, the Prime Minister, Henry John Temple, Viscount Palmerston, died after an illness of but a few days. Palmerston had been either Foreign Secretary or Premier in a succession of Whig governments before 1859, at which time, under difficult circumstances, he again became Prime Minister. Earlier in 1865, he had been endorsed, once more, by the electors and had proved himself without a doubt the most popular politician of his day. His funeral was an elaborate state affair. A blanket of melancholy seemed to hang over the entire city. The West End shops were closed, business was suspended in the City of London, all the ships upon the Thames had flags at half-mast, and the funeral path was

lined with what the London papers regarded as the largest
number of spectators since the burial of the Duke of Wel-
lington. The long procession moved wearily over the
cobblestones until finally it arrived at the Abbey of Westminster where the Prime Minister's remains received
stately burial.

Palmerston's aggressive patriotism had made him the
darling of the English public and a villain for the Radicals.
His high-handed behaviour in defence of British citizens
in foreign parts had roused imperial Britain to cheer
loudly, and for many years, when troubled by the slightest
difficulty abroad, British travellers were known to snap
that 'Lord Palmerston shall hear of this.' Now, Palmerston,
the one fixed point in the politics of his time, was dead
and the stage was set for a new patterning. English politics
in 1865 had no stability. Personalities rather than issues
were crucial and the Palmerston name had had a special
magic: Sidney Herbert had even suggested that Palmerston was 'the only public man in England who has a name.'
The Viscount's interests had been almost exclusively in
foreign affairs. He had revealed his attitude towards matters domestic when asked, before the opening of Parliament in 1864, what the Queen's speech would say on home
legislation. Rubbing his hands with obvious satisfaction, he
had answered, 'Oh, there is really nothing to be done. We
cannot go on adding to the Statute Book *ad infinitum.*
Perhaps we may have a little law reform, or bankruptcy
reform; but we cannot go on legislating forever.' The Radical wing of Palmerston's own party—with a full programme of domestic reforms ready for use—found itself
blocked. When Palmerston died, new life was injected
into British politics. Most particularly, there was a revival
of interest in the cause of electoral reform, of which Palmerston had been the most steadfast opponent.

The Reform Bill of 1832 which had given the vote to
the middle classes had brought about no real change in
the structure of the governing cabinet. But in the House
of Commons, there now was a group of middle-class Radicals, destined, in time to come, to play a leading role in
the shaping of Liberal policy, men who felt that they

represented the best sense of the country and its best interests, but found themselves outnumbered by the representatives of the aristocracy and gentry—the owners of landed property. The Radical programme—of the new class of factory-owners—was based upon the system of political economy outlined by Adam Smith and David Ricardo, and its prime dictum was *laissez-faire*: let government—and Tory factory reformers—keep hands off business. Radicalism worked to eliminate the special economic and political privileges and the government sinecures, long held by the landowners. They worked towards a reformation of the tax structure so that the indirect taxes which had been placed upon industry and trade would be replaced by direct taxes on landed property. They wished to reform the educational system. The Radicals were passionately devoted to international peace: war caused economic dislocation—and was unchristian—and both Bright and Cobden had staunchly opposed Palmerston's aggressive policies, deaf to appeals to 'national honour' which they regarded as feudal and obsolete. They opposed 'excessive' expenditure on the army and navy, and on colonies. The Radicals—in whose numbers dissenters were prominently represented—had strong doubts about the maintenance of the Established Church. Yet, how were the Radicals to dislodge the landed aristocracy from the seats of power and carry their programme? The Radical leadership realized that there was no alternative to extending the suffrage still further and allying themselves with a newly enfranchised working class. That this was a dangerous business, they fully understood, yet it was a risk which they believed they had to take. In seeking this, they joined forces with a working class which had set its heart on universal suffrage as early as the 'thirties.

The fight for Reform was to centre about John Bright—whose position in English politics was not too unlike that of George Gordon in the politics of Jamaica. The son of a Quaker millowner, Bright had been one of the most active campaigners for the repeal of the Corn Laws. A friend of the impoverished Irish, a leading advocate of the abolition of flogging in the army, an opponent of the Crimean War, Bright's frequent attacks upon the established order made the more conservative of the middle classes regard him as a red Republican, a dangerous demagogue who did not hesitate to endanger the lives and property of the 'respectable' classes and the liberties guaranteed by the British constitution by stirring up class antagonism. During the 'sixties, Bright was to become the most hated and most feared man in the country.

In the 'fifties and 'sixties, many members of the middle classes had become increasingly frightened at the prospect of universal suffrage. The election of 1857 had revealed a shift away from the more Radical wing of Liberalism, and numbers of voters who had previously supported the Radicals, now had begun to vote either for more conservative Liberals or for Tories. Middle-class fears of a working-class electorate increased after the Crimean War, when a great strike movement began. Between 1859 and 1861, the builders' union in London struck for a nine-hour day, and the whole of the organized labour movement lent its support—a demonstration of a united working-class, growing more conscious of its power and ready and able to use its new-found strength, which appalled the middle and upper classes. To much of the public, the reform campaign and this trade union agitation seemed cut from the same cloth. They were part of the new onrush towards democracy. The victory of the North during the American Civil War added to the fearful conviction of English respectability that democracy—the democracy espoused by Bright in parliament and by Mill in his writings—might be politically imminent.

The American Civil War, which had begun in 1861, had revealed the sharp division in British opinion which was to be so apparent in the Eyre case. The bulk of the upper and middle classes favoured the South. Britons had long been accustomed to viewing with favour wars waged by suppressed nationalities, and, for many Englishmen, the Civil War seemed a fight for 'Southern Independence.' To many British Free Traders, the war appeared to be a fight over tariffs, with the South adopting a 'correct' low tariff position against the North's attempts to impose high protective duties. The Civil War, furthermore, caused economic dislocation in the textile factories of Lancashire which were starved for the raw cotton and only a Southern victory could get raw cotton back and quickly. Pro-Southern English gentlemen denied that slavery was really an issue in the war, and this view was rather easy to defend in the years before the issuance of the Emancipation Proclamation. Others, including the highly regarded Carlyle, felt sympathetic to the institution of slavery, considering it superior to the 'wage-slavery' of the factories. The Southern conception of 'aristocratic' government, furthermore, was more congenial to the upper and upper-middle classes than was the republican democracy of the North. The Radicals, on the other hand, supported the North just because they sympathized with its democratic institutions and because they—and the Exeter Hall groups —were the most steadfast opponents of slavery.

One of these Radicals was the philosopher of liberty, John Stuart Mill. In his *Autobiography*, Mill wrote:

> My strongest feelings were engaged in this struggle, which, I felt from the beginning, was destined to be a turning point, for good or evil, of the course of human affairs for an indefinite duration. . . . Their [the South's] success, if they succeeded, would be a victory of the powers of evil which would give courage to the enemies of progress and damp the spirits of its friends all over the civilized world, while it would create a formidable military power, grounded on the worst and most anti-social form of the tyranny of men over men, and, by destroying for a long time the prestige of the great democratic republic, would give to all the privileged classes of Europe a false confidence, probably only to be extinguished in blood.

Mill had been horrified by 'the rush of nearly the whole upper and middle classes of my own country, even those who passed for Liberals, into a furious pro-Southern partisanship,' and regretted that the generation which had freed the West Indian slaves had passed away. 'I never

before felt so keenly,' Mill concluded, 'how little permanent improvement had reached the minds of our influential classes, and of what small value were the Liberal
opinions they had got into the habit of professing.' But
Mill was not alone. The British working class, too, supported the North—this even in Lancashire where the cotton
famine had caused unemployment. There was also a small
group of Radical barristers, literary men, and scholars, all
democrats, all defenders of the North. Tom Hughes
joined his Christian Socialist colleague of Chartist days,
J. M. Ludlow, in writing in favour of the North. Both,
incidentally, were also deeply involved in the legal defence of trade unionism. John Bright spoke for the North
in the House of Commons and on political platforms
throughout the nation.

In 1862, these Radicals formed an Emancipation Society
in London to back the Northern cause. Among the members of this London group were many whom we shall
soon meet again—Mill, Hughes, Peter Taylor, Professor
Cairnes, Godfrey Lushington, Edward Miall, Professor
Beesly, Edward Dicey, Edmond Beales and Jacob Bright.
Although the London society was not without accomplish-
ments, the most active of the pro-Northern Societies in
England was the famous Union and Emancipation Society
of Manchester. It, too, worked valiantly throughout the
course of the war to enlist public opinion on the Northern
side.

Goldwin Smith, a prominent Radical and the Regius
Professor of Modern History at Oxford, had been in the
forefront of the advocates of the North during the Civil
War. On 18th October 1865, before the news of the Jamaican uprising had become known in England, Smith
wrote to an American friend, C. E. Norton, a letter in
which he sympathized with the grave problem which the
Negro freedman posed for the United States. 'How can
there be real political equality without social fusion,' he
asked; 'and how can there be social fusion while the difference of colour and the physical antipathy remain?' Smith
then suggested the solution of American 'Negro emigra-
tion on a large scale' to the British West Indies. 'Happily,'

Smith wrote, 'our West Indian dependencies under a really paternal government (for such, say what you will, the British government in dependencies is) lie close at hand.' In this letter, Smith also wrote of his fears that all Europe, following the example of France under Napoleon III, was in danger of sinking under 'military despotisms.' The news of the Jamaican massacre was to alter Goldwin Smith's opinion of British paternalism in the West Indies, and to reinforce his fears of military despotism. Writing to Norton once more, on 1st January 1866, Smith declared that 'no feature' of the Jamaican controversy 'is more terrible— I might say appalling—than the sympathy which our military men in this country almost unanimously display with the violence and atrocity of their brethren in Jamaica. Heaven grant that we may never fall under their yoke. But it is a danger to which we ought not to be blind.'

It was in a speech to a self-satisfied valedictory meeting of the Manchester Emancipation Society, early in 1866, that Goldwin Smith forged the link between the advocates of the North in the Civil War and a new group whose aim was to be the prosecution of Governor Eyre. Smith told the meeting that the most serious problem which the United States was then facing was the reorganization of Southern society, adding that 'Jamaica tells us with terrible emphasis what are the perils of a community composed of the ex-slave owner and the ex-slave.' Smith expressed his regret that 'the territorial aristocracy of this country and the clergy of the Established Church should vehemently sympathize' with the slave power. 'Conservatives must not think,' he added, 'that they can sanction violence till the law is settled in their own favour, and thenceforth permit it no more. . . . This is no superfluous remark, when that strange and fearful epilogue to the Civil War in America, the Jamaica Massacre, is about to become the subject of a party contest.'

As early as December 1865, moves had been taken to unite those who wished to defend the interests of the West Indian Negroes, Exeter Hall Societies, and Radical groups, into a 'Jamaica Committee.' In the list of the Jamaica Committee's officers, executive members, and rank and file, we find virtually all of the leading figures in the two principal pro-Northern societies. Having triumphed in their support of one struggle for democracy and against slavery across the seas, these gentlemen were willing to fight for the same principles at home. The chairman of the new Committee was Charles Buxton, M.P., the son of the famous Thomas Fowell Buxton who had carried emancipation to its victory in 1833. Since the new Jamaica Committee was to stage its activities in London, the officers of the recently dissolved London Emancipation Society took immediate responsibility for its affairs. Peter Taylor, a Unitarian Member of Parliament for Leicester and a partner in the famous firm of silk merchants, Samuel Courtauld and Co., had served as the Treasurer of the London Emancipation Society, and also assumed this office for the new Committee. F. W. Chesson, a young man in his early thirties who was to devote the remainder of his life to a succession of humanitarian enterprises, had been the Emancipation Society's Secretary, and also served as the Secretary of the Committee.

The two most famous of the early members of the Committee were Thomas Hughes and John Stuart Mill. Hughes, best known as the author of *Tom Brown's Schooldays*, personified the ethic instilled at Rugby by Dr Arnold, that of Christian manliness (stimulated by cold showers) and 'playing the game.' In his early twenties, Hughes was converted to democracy: 'I was rapidly falling away from the political faith in which we had been brought up,' he wrote; 'the noble side of democracy was carrying me away'; in 1848, he made his way to Christian Socialism. In the years preceding the Jamaica insurrection, Hughes had been one of the early promoters of a Workingmen's College in London as well as a legal defender of trade unionism. In 1865, he decided to go into politics and had been elected a Member of Parliament for Lambeth.

In the parliamentary elections of July 1865, held just before Palmerston's death, John Stuart Mill, the economist and philosopher, was the Liberal candidate in the City of Westminster, seeking election upon a platform of extending the suffrage, and he, too, had been victorious. Mill's victory was significant, bringing the foremost philosophic champion of democracy to the national senate. Unlike a great many of his Radical colleagues, Mill was not a nonconformist, not even, most probably, a Christian. Not wealthy, he lived on a pension, a quite adequate one, provided by the East India Company which he had served for many years. Mill felt more moved by the events in Jamaica than by the American Civil War: he could not stand aside and let pass without protest 'excesses of authority as revolting as any of those for which, when perpetrated by instruments of other Governments, Englishmen can hardly find terms sufficient to express their abhorrence.' In the first year of what was to be his only parliament—his long service with the East India Company had precluded any active role in politics up to his retirement—Mill was closely watched by the more usual politicians, unaccustomed to seeing an intellectual in their midst. He, in turn, long denied the opportunity to take a forthright public stand on political questions, sought a cause to compensate for his long enforced silence and found it in the case of Governor Eyre.

There were, in all, nineteen Members of Parliament who were members of the Jamaica Committee. The list must of course be headed by the Reform leader in the House of Commons, John Bright, who shrewdly recognized the importance of the Jamaica business and its significance to the cause of reform. There were three baronets, all Members of Parliament, among the 300 prominent members of the Committee, but the title of baronet had more and more, at this time, become a middle-class distinction generally awarded for success in commerce. These included Sir Samuel Morton Peto, the wealthy Baptist contractor who represented Bristol; the noted carpet manufacturer, Congregationalist, and philanthropist, Sir Francis Crossley; and Sir Thomas Fowell Buxton, the elder brother of the Committee's chairman, Charles Buxton, and the heir of the leader of the fight for emancipation. Samuel Morley, a wealthy Nottingham hosierer and a pious Congregationalist, the treasurer of the Home Missionary Society, a temperance leader, and a fervent supporter of Bright, who had been elected Liberal M.P. for Nottingham, was an active member. Instead of dukes, earls, marquises, and viscounts—there were no members of the House of Lords upon the Committee—the Jamaica Committee had *clergymen*; thirty-two of the original 300 members of the Committee were ministers. Most of the members of the Committee came either from the capital or from the big industrial cities, from Glasgow, Manchester, Birmingham, Leeds, Bradford, Bristol, Liverpool, and Reading, rather than from the rural counties. In a word, the members of the Jamaica Committee were men of the new middle classes, sober, respectable, pious and serious.

Typical of the rank-and-file members were such men as the Reverend William Anderson, known as 'daft Willie Anderson,' a supporter of the Poles, and Italians and other suppressed nationalities and a fervent opponent of the established church; Edward Miall, a Congregational minister, who had in 1841, established a weekly journal, the *Nonconformist*, which waged all-out war against high-church, Anglo-Catholic tendencies in the Church of England, at whose disestablishment it aimed (in the 'forties Miall had joined the Chartists in advocating universal manhood suffrage, and had tried to reconcile the differences between the working-class and middle-class Radicalism); Henry James Slack, the editor of a paper called the *Intellectual Observer*, a Unitarian in religion, a Radical Cobdenite in politics, formerly active in the anti-slavery movement, and a warm friend of both Mazzini and Kossuth; Benjamin Scott, a fervent Congregationalist and temperance advocate, a financial expert—as Chamberlain of the City of London, his acumen saved the corporation of the city from even a penny's loss in the Black Friday panic of 1866; Professor Francis William Newman, the brother of Cardinal Newman, was a Unitarian and a Radical, and held the chair of Latin in University College, London, where he used as textbooks Latin translations he himself had made of *Hiawatha* and *Robinson Crusoe*. Professor John Eliot Cairnes, one of the leading economists in the United Kingdom, a loyal friend and disciple of Mill, was professor of political economy in University College,

London, and an earnest member; so was Edward Baines, the Liberal M.P. for Leeds, an earnest Congregationalist, a former editor of the Leeds *Mercury*, and a historian of some distinction. Another adherent of the Jamaica Committee was Edward Dicey, a young and promising journalist, who wrote leading articles for the *Daily Telegraph*. Thomas Bayley Potter, a Unitarian who had succeeded to Cobden's seat at Rochdale at the latter's death in 1865, was Manchester-born, his father and uncle were among the founders of the *Manchester Guardian,* and he had served as president of the Union and Emancipation Society of that city, before transferring his interests to the Eyre case.

This then was the character of the committee members: radical in politics, non-conformist in religion, men whose ties were to middle-class business enterprise, rather than to the land; professors, journalists, political economists, non-conformist ministers. They were men who had given themselves in the past to similar causes: the advocacy of the North during the Civil War; the support of Kossuth and Mazzini, of Hungarian and Italian nationalism; and, most important at this time, men committed to the cause of universal suffrage. The Committee had no working-class members. It was such a body of men who—while awaiting the report of the Royal Commission—were determined to make effective use of the events in Jamaica to further their overall political principles and objectives.

The full Royal Commission of three members met for the first time on the island of Jamaica on the 20th of January, and five days later, began the laborious process of taking evidence. In the following months, many hundreds of Jamaicans gave their testimony at the hearings at the government quarters at Spanish Town. On a number of occasions, the Commissioners, either jointly or individually, went on circuit to Morant Bay, or to Stony Gut, or to Monklands, to take evidence at the scene of disturbances. They sat over sixty times during a period of fifty-one days, and 730 witnesses were heard. There had been many difficulties. Many of the witnesses were uneducated, with little notion of what constituted 'evidence,' and were very vague indeed when questioned about specific details. The Commissioners, furthermore, professed to have had trouble understanding the soft accent of the Jamaican Negroes. Sometimes witnesses presented obvious tall tales. On other occasions, more reasonable stories, when checked on the scene, proved wholly untrue. Many of the blacks thought that the Commissioners had come to receive claims for property damage and deliberately exaggerated. Even 'educated' witnesses, both black and white, had to be constantly cautioned by the Commissioners to testify as to the facts, not to retail hearsay or private views and prejudices. A mountain of testimony was accumulated, filling, ultimately, several thousand printed pages.

The Commissioners made a careful investigation of the origins of the outbreak, both the troubles of October 1865 and the long feud between Eyre and Gordon. They heard from Governor Eyre and from his commanders in the field. Colonel Hobbs' testimony had been especially disconcerting. Though his dispatches had been the most horrifying, it developed that the Colonel had been largely boasting of his atrociousness. What he had actually done—although frightening enough—had been considerably less than what he had said he had done. A letter, written to Hobbs by the Adjutant General, requesting the Colonel to act ruthlessly and not burden the army by keeping prisoners alive, was placed in evidence. The Colonel had understood what was expected of him and had acted accordingly, embroidering his reports with stories of floggings, shootings, hangings in order to curry favour. Other officers, it turned out, had done much the same, though not so systematically. They, too, wished to appear good fellows to their superiors and to the bloodthirsty planters, shivering fearfully in Kingston. The Commissioners uncovered evidence which led them to take a dim view of the way in which the courts martial were conducted, especially that of Gordon. They concluded that Gordon seemed not to have been involved in the conspiracy, the crime for which he had been executed, but asserted that Paul Bogle had been

inflamed by Gordon's words and believed himself to have
been following Gordon's real if unexpressed wishes.

The testimony was carefully sifted and discussed for
many weeks, and on 9th April 1866, the report was ready.
The Commissioners had reached several conclusions. They
were fully convinced that the outbreak at St Thomas, had
been a planned resistance to authority whose object was
to secure royal lands free of rent, that this insurrection
had been motivated by Negro distrust of planter-
dominated courts, and that some of the conspirators, at
least, wished to drive the whites from the island. They
further agreed that there had been a genuine danger of
the spread of the insurrection if the Morant Bay uprising
had been more successful. They therefore concluded:

> That praise is due to Governor Eyre for the skill, promp-
> titude, and vigour which he manifested during the
> early stages of the insurrection; to the exercise of which
> qualities its speedy termination is in a great degree to
> be attributed.
> That the Military and Naval operations appear to us
> to have been prompt and judicious.

To these words of praise, however, were added the following qualifications:

> That by the continuance of martial law in its full force
> to the extreme limit of its statutory operation the people
> were deprived for a longer than the necessary period
> of the great constitutional privileges by which the se-
> curity of life and property is provided for.
> Lastly. That the punishments inflicted were excessive.
>   (1) That the punishment of death was unneces-
>   sarily frequent.
>   (2) That the floggings were reckless, and at Bath
>   positively barbarous.
>   (3) That the burning of 1000 houses was wanton
>   and cruel.
> All of which we humbly submit to Your Majesty's
> gracious consideration.

It was several weeks before the report could reach the Colonial Office and still more time elapsed before publication. When 'the facts' which the British public had so long awaited finally became known, the effect was electrifying. The verification of many of the atrocity stories which the Governor's early supporters had denounced as impossible fabrications was most shocking, and the defenders of Eyre were hurled back upon the defensive. Most prominent among early defenders of the Governor had been the London *Times*. Having been in the forefront of those who had pooh-poohed the 'wild' stories of the previous December, it was doubly stunned by the evidence.

There is no longer any reasonable doubt [the *Times* reported] that cruelties, of which it is impossible to think without shuddering, were perpetrated in the suppression of the Jamaica insurrection.

Once again, meetings were held to denounce the 'wholesale murderer of Jamaica.' Emotions at an anti-Eyre meeting at Brighton ran so high that one gentleman who had dared to say a word in favour of the Governor was firmly and none too gently escorted from the hall. Special attention was riveted upon the execution of Gordon. At a demonstration at Exeter Hall shortly after the Comsion's report had been made public, copies of Gordon's last letter to his wife were distributed at the door. The letter, printed on black-edged paper, was well calculated to touch the hearts of Exeter Hall audiences.

After the publication of the report of the Royal Commission in early June, the Jamaica Committee, which had been anxiously awaiting it, divided sharply as to the next step. One group felt that the committee had done everything possible in obtaining the reprimand and recall of Eyre—what more could it hope for? Another more militant segment wished to prosecute the ex-Governor of Jamaica for the murder of Gordon—feeling that unless this were done, his behaviour would serve as an encouragement for others. The controversy reached a climax at a meeting of the Executive Committee on 26th June 1866. The Chairman, Charles Buxton, headed the faction which regarded a prosecution of Eyre for murder as an enormous error. Finding himself, however, unable to attend the meeting, Buxton wrote a letter presenting his views to the Secretary. 'No one, indeed,' Buxton's letter began, 'can have felt a deeper indignation than myself at the shameful misconduct of Governor Eyre.' But the question under discussion was whether Eyre should be prosecuted for *murder*. Buxton was convinced that 'Eyre was under the belief that a widespread conspiracy had broken out in the island with a view to a general massacre of the white population; and that his conduct, therefore, while 'shameful and criminal,' did not involve him in the 'guilt of wilful murder.' 'Our common sense,' Buxton argued, 'will not permit us to blind ourselves to the truth that we could not possibly injure our own cause more than by such a prosecution.' Even if a grand jury should indict Eyre, a trial jury would probably not convict him. Even if convicted, did anyone doubt that he would receive a royal pardon? 'Under any one of these three contingencies, he would be regarded by public opinion as a martyr who had been vindictively and cruelly assailed; and his escape from danger would be hailed as a glorious triumph for himself and his partisans.' What ought to be done, Buxton suggested was to secure the 'dismissal and disgrace' of Eyre's confederates and to get compensation for those who had been injured by the outrages.

Buxton's position on the question was shared by a number of others including the chairman's elder brother, Sir Thomas Fowell Buxton. Buxton concluded his letter by offering to resign as chairman if the majority of the Committee felt it necessary to prosecute. The meeting took place as scheduled and Buxton's letter was read to the members. There was much heated discussion. John Stuart Mill, strongly supported by John Bright, was the most forceful advocate of prosecution. This was a matter he was determined to see through to its end, he asserted. If Eyre were not prosecuted, Mill argued, every rascally colonial official would be given a free hand to perform mischief,

and a horrible precedent affecting the liberties of Englishmen would be set. These arguments proved convincing.
A decision was reached that the Committee would move
either to have the government prosecute Eyre, or, acting
through Mrs Gordon, who had recently come to London
to live, would prosecute the Governor itself.

Word of this decision was announced in the Radical
press, which, however, made no mention of any Committee opposition, whereupon Buxton sent a copy of his letter
to the *Times* for publication. His aim, as he told the paper,
was to make his position clear to a public which might
otherwise think that he, the chairman, had agreed with
the view of the majority. There was considerable annoy-
ance among the other members of the committee. Mill
and John Bright, especially, believed Buxton had not behaved properly in placing private committee business on
public exhibition, and were disturbed at the effect the
letter might have upon Mrs Gordon, whose co-operation
they deemed essential, and who was already quite hesitant
about joining in a prosecution for murder. This fear proved
justified. Soon after Buxton's letter had been published,
Mrs Gordon wrote to the Committee: 'I shrink from the
step suggested. My martyred husband, shaping his course
in public and in private life by his Christian profession,
died forgiving his enemies. I leave Mr Eyre and those
who have aided him in his cruel proceedings in the hands
of "Him who judgest righteously."'

On Monday, 9th July 1866, a special meeting of the
Jamaica Committee was called at Radley's Hotel, London;
the public and the press were invited to attend, and
Buxton was asked to be present. The meeting's obsten-
sible purpose was to select a new chairman. Its real purpose was to publicly rebuke Charles Buxton, who it was
felt, had violated his gentlemanly obligations to his
associates. Peter Taylor, the Committee's Treasurer, began the attack, accusing Buxton of having severely
damaged the prestige of the Committee and of having
swayed Mrs Gordon, whom, nonetheless, Taylor praised
for her feelings, which 'did her credit.' The Jamaica Committee, Taylor continued, was not motivated by any

desire for vengeance. Governor Eyre as a person was nothing to the Committee—'he was simply the personification of wrong.' John Bright next wielded the cudgel. While not denying that Buxton had been most generous in the past, having given the Committee not only leadership but financial support, Buxton had now, at the point where they could do some real good, backed out and 'left them all in the lurch.' The Governor and the other Jamaica 'criminals' had to be brought to the bar of a criminal court, Bright insisted, if future colonial governors were to have a proper respect for human life. Edmond Beales, the middle-class barrister who headed the working-class suffrage organization, the Reform League, warned that unless Eyre were prosecuted, 'there would be a strong feeling throughout the country that there was one law for the rich and another for the poor.' Buxton defended himself with some ability, repeating his previous arguments against prosecution, but without success.

The next order of business was the selection of a new chairman. To no one's surprise, and amid great applause, John Stuart Mill was unanimously elected. The handsome, white-haired old man rose to respond to this tribute. 'Gentlemen,' he began, 'I thank you for this honour and mark of your confidence. I accept the post you have given me. I do so in the full conviction that the objects of this committee are simply to ascertain whether there exist in this country any means for making a British functionary responsible for blood unlawfully shed, and whether that be murder or not. I believe it to be murder.' There were shouts of 'hear, hear' from the members. 'This committee ought not to rest,' Mill concluded, 'until it obtains from the Legislature the assurance that men like Mr Eyre will be made responsible for their criminal actions.' The Jamaica Committee's next move, then, was to be made in parliament.

The chief business which faced the Russell government during the spring of 1866 had been Reform. Palmerston's death during the previous October made it certain that the advocates of reform were going to press hard to extend the suffrage. Russell had been in the Liberal cabinet which had, in 1832, given the vote to the middle classes and he had strongly advocated that measure as the 'final' word on the franchise. Now important sections of his party urged him to make Reform truly 'final' by admitting the workingman to the vote, though a no less influential group of Liberals—led by Robert Lowe—was unalterably against such a change, which, they believed, would result in the destruction of constitutional liberty and the undermining of private property. Russell, torn between the two views, at last determined that his government would present a bill. The process of framing such a bill and securing its passage had been understandably difficult. So when, in June, the House of Lords rejected the government's Reform Bill, Russell decided that he had had enough. He resigned and turned the government over to the Conservatives rather than call a new election which he might have won, thus finding himself once again with the problem of suffrage reform. In June 1866, Britain had a new government: Earl Derby was the Prime Minister and Benjamin Disraeli, the Chancellor of the Exchequer. Furious at the turn of events, the Radicals publicly denounced both the Tories and the House of Lords, and privately denounced Russell for having given way without further struggle. Though faced with a Tory government, which they felt would be much more difficult to win over to Reform, they nevertheless were determined to see the fight through. Different tactics would of course be necessary in dealing with a Tory government and the Radicals were perfectly prepared to use almost any means to gain their goal.

The Radical leaders of the Jamaica Committee also determined to switch tactics in the House of Commons now that there was a Tory government. For them, too, the new course was all-out attack. Previously, the case of Governor Eyre had been kept out of parliamentary discussion. Even after the publication of the Commission report, the Radicals had refrained from embarrassing the Liberal government, most especially since it was involved in Reform legislation. But they were perfectly willing to assault

Earl Derby's government, and the nineteen M.P. members
of the Jamaica Committee felt they could make a good
showing in a parliamentary debate. Ten days after John
Stuart Mill had announced his intentions of securing 'from
the Legislature the assurance that men like Mr Eyre will
be made responsible for their criminal actions,' on Thursday, 19th July 1866, Mill himself opened the parliamentary attack on Governor Eyre by asking the Chancellor
of the Exchequer, after a recital of the Jamaica atrocities,
'whether any legal proceedings have been or will be
ordered to be taken against Mr Edward John Eyre, lately
Governor of Jamaica, for complicity in all or any of the
above acts, and particularly for the illegal trial and execution of Mr George William Gordon: and, if not,
whether Her Majesty's Government are advised that these
acts are not offences under the Criminal Law?' Disraeli, in
reply, criticized Mill for unfairly assuming guilt before
trial and reminded the new chairman of the Jamaica
Committee that the acts of which he complained had
taken place under the operation of martial law. The previous government, Disraeli noted, had carefully examined
all the facts, had ordered Eyre's dismissal, and had referred the cases of his subordinates to the proper government departments, the Admiralty and the Horse Guards.
Certainly, the Tory government could do nothing further.
Was not Mill, the Chancellor asked in conclusion, con-
fusing 'errors of conduct and errors of judgment with
malice prepense?'

On July 31st, a full-blown parliamentary attack upon
Governor Eyre was launched—though, surprisingly, not by
Mill but by the recently cashiered chairman of the Jamaica
Committee, Charles Buxton. Buxton, although unwilling to
join the prosecution of Eyre for murder, was determined to
obtain a parliamentary censure of the Governor's conduct,
and initiated a day-long debate in the House, for whose
consideration he presented four resolutions. The first
deplored the excessive punishments imposed during the
suppression of the disturbances in Jamaica. The second
called for punishment of the perpetrators of these excesses.
The third asked the government to award compensation

'to those whose property was wantonly and cruelly destroyed, and to the families of those who were put to death illegally.' The fourth asked for remission of all further punishment upon Jamaicans still in custody. 'No one,' Buxton argued, 'need fear that in supporting these Resolutions that he would run any risk of hampering or increasing the responsibility of any Governor or other official who might have to deal with any insurrection that might arise on future occasions,' for Buxton's resolutions did not refer to the conduct of British officials or soldiers during the repression. What concerned him were the punishments inflicted after the disturbances had been suppressed and the authority of the Government restored.

Buxton listed the atrocities committed after October 20th, when the danger had definitely passed, in a long and painful catalogue. His expostulation upon the guilt of the young men, like Herbert Brand, who composed the courts martial at Morant Bay, was most moving:

> I would a thousand times rather have followed a son of mine to the grave [he proclaimed] than have had him sit as a member of that court martial, and have shown himself so lost to every feeling not only of humanity, but of personal honour—so dead to every generous youthful impulse—as to have stooped to the utter degradation of being merely the executioner, the hangman, the base instrument used by the authorities for consigning these 400 trembling wretches to the whipping post and the gallows.

'The broad question is whether the people of England approve or condemn the deeds I have described,' Buxton stated in conclusion:

> The whole country and the whole of Christendom, which has looked on with more interest at this matter than is perhaps generally known, will fully understand that the question on which we shall divide is simply as to whether England will or will not sanction these butcheries. I await that decision with the deepest anxiety. It

would, indeed, be a blow to the cause of humanity,
it would indeed be a dark stain on the character of the
British people, should the House bestow its sanction
upon such doings. I trust that the party to which I
belong will refuse to identify itself with them.

Turning to the Conservative benches, Buxton asked
whether those gentlemen believed the Jamaican authorities had adopted the course of wisdom or the course of
vengeance. 'Do they regard it as an example to be followed by authorities elsewhere, or one to be repudiated
and abhorred?' Buxton implored the Conservatives 'to
trample underfoot mere prejudice and party feeling, and
to ask themselves solemnly, whether, as the Government
and representatives of the British people, they dare, in the
face of the world and in the face of Heaven, to stamp the
seal of deliberate approval on these ruthless deeds.'
    There was silence in the House as Buxton resumed his
seat. Tories, who had believed him a dangerous tool of the
Radical extremists when he agreed to head the Jamaica
Committee, had come once more to regard him as a man
of principle when he refused to countenance the prosecution of Eyre for murder. His present indictment of Eyre
therefore seemed stronger in the light of his recent conflict
with his former colleagues of the Jamaica Committee.
    However, the Buxton address was answered on behalf
of the government by the Under-Secretary for the Colonies,
Charles Adderley, who proceeded to accuse Buxton of
having behaved dishonestly in proposing that the House
pick out of the Commission's report all the censures and
omit all the praises of Governor Eyre. Was there any class
of servants of the Crown with a more difficult task than
those placed at distant and often unhealthy stations and
confronted by most trying circumstances, in which they
must act upon their own judgment at a moment's notice?
'Are they of all men to be treated with the scantiest
justice?' This was a great imperial problem, Adderley declared, and he appealed to Buxton 'as a man who has an
interest in the Colonial Empire of England,' whether it
ought not to be 'the policy of a great Empire, to put the

most favourable construction' upon such action?' 'It is not
every man who is able so to hold the scales of justice
through the difficulties of a terrible crisis; and let me tell
you, that if you always expect these rare qualities to be
displayed by every Governor, you will find it no easy
matter to get men to undertake Colonial Governorships.'
The Jamaica Committee, he proclaimed, had decided,
even before the committee of inquiry had reported the
evidence, that Governor Eyre was a murderer. 'Strong pre-
possessions, invincible prejudices incapacitated as well as
disciplined them from seeing more than one side' of the
question, and what was significant was that 'they prefer to
range themselves on the side of those who are disturbers
of order, rather than on the side of those who have upheld it.' The government moved the rejection of the
Buxton resolutions.

The friends of Governor Eyre, heartened by this spirited
defence, rushed to support the Under-Secretary. One
asked why there was no sympathy for the whites who had
died in the rebellion? It might have been supposed that
the whole nation would sympathize with Governor Eyre
and his officers (as they had sympathized with the victims
and avengers of the terrible Indian mutiny); but public
opinion had been manufactured on the subject, and instead
of sympathy, meetings were held to expose Eyre to
ridicule and contempt. Eyre was a 'humane and honourable' man, but, even if this were not so, it would still have
been the duty of the Government to support an officer
placed in such a high and responsible position. There were
murmurs of approval throughout the House. A Tory,
Colonel North, who was to be a chief spokesman for the
Eyre cause, also rushed to Adderley's support. North
particularly resented Buxton's criticisms of the military and
naval forces, piously intoning that 'if there was one feeling
more conspicuously displayed than another by English
officers generally, whether belonging to the army or the
navy, it was that of extreme humanity, and nothing could
be more painful to a British officer than to be called upon
to perform anything like an act of cruelty.' Even the
former Liberal Colonial minister spoke on Eyre's behalf.

Cardwell described the ex-Governor as a man of courage and humanity faced with a difficult and terrifying situation. It was impossible not to deplore the undue continuance of martial law and the excessive executions and floggings, Cardwell added; but if it was a grievous fault, 'I have reason to know that the punishment which has fallen upon Governor Eyre has been deeply felt.'

The former Liberal Under-Secretary for the Colonies, W. E. Forster, spoke in a rather different vein. Perhaps because of earlier sympathies and family connections with Radicalism, Forster laid emphasis upon the excessive executions and punishments. Some 354 persons had been 'legally massacred.' Even the repressions of the continental despotisms, Forster asserted, including the Russian behaviour in Poland and the Austrian suppression of the Hungarian revolution, dreadful as they had been, had not resulted in so many executions with so little justification on the grounds of either justice or military necessity. Yet, Forster felt, Eyre had had no 'bad motives' and could not rightly be charged with murder. How was it that a humane and conscientious man like Eyre had sanctioned and that British officers had perpetrated atrocities from which they would have shrunk had their victims been white men, Forster inquired. The answer was simple: they were not free from a feeling of contempt for what they regarded as an inferior race. This made it all the more important for parliament, which could sit calmly in judgment, to affirm that there ought not be more than one code of morality. Ferocity towards black men was as evil and as unwise as towards white. The fault was not that of an individual as of a feeling to which we are all tempted in dealing with weaker races. Therefore, said Forster, he wished the House to protest against the proceedings in Jamaica, and to condemn that misuse of strength to which there was always a temptation.

Thomas Hughes, the newly elected M.P. for Lambeth, rose to assert that if the country allowed the deeds done in Jamaica to pass without judicial review, they would be the first generation of Englishmen to shirk the duty of seeing that the honour of England did not come to disgrace in the hands of persons who represented her in the colonies. Were he, Hughes, in Eyre's position, the Radical barrister concluded, he would insist upon a trial as the only method of consulting the honour and interests of England committed to his charge.

Finally, John Stuart Mill, got to his feet. His speech was brief but eloquent, and he was later to describe it as 'the best of my speeches in parliament.' The Royal Commission, he began, had shown that the lives of subjects of Her Majesty had been wrongfully taken and that the persons of other subjects had been grossly maltreated:

> I maintain that when such things have been done, there is a *prima facie* demand for legal punishment, and that a court of criminal justice can alone determine whether such punishment has been merited, and if merited, what ought to be its amount. The taking of human lives without justification, which in this case is an admitted fact, cannot be condoned by anything short of a criminal tribunal. Neither the Government, nor this House, nor the whole English nation combined, can exercise a pardoning power without previous trial and sentence.

If officers of the Government are to be allowed to take the lives of the Queen's subjects improperly without being called to account and having the excuses they make sifted and adjudicated by the courts, 'we are giving up altogether the principle of government by law, and resigning ourselves to arbitrary power.'

> I do not deny that there is good authority, legal as well as military, for saying that the proclamation of martial law suspends all law so long as it lasts; but I defy any one to produce any respectable authority for the doctrine that persons are not responsible to the laws of their country, both civil and criminal, after martial law has ceased, for acts done under it. . . . [Indeed] if martial law . . . is what it is asserted to be, arbitrary power—the rule of force, subject to no legal limits—then, indeed, the legal responsibility of those who administer

it, instead of being lightened, requires to be enormously aggravated. . . . When there is absolutely no guarantee against any extreme of tyrannical violence, but the responsibility which can be afterwards exacted from the tyrant—then, Sir, it is indeed indispensable that he who takes the lives of others under this discretion should know that he risks his own.

'We want to know,' Mill concluded, 'who are to be our masters: the Queen's Judges and a jury of our countrymen, administering the laws of England, or three military or naval officers, two of them boys, administering, as the Chancellor of the Exchequer tells us, no law at all.' 'It remains to be seen whether the people of England will support us in the attempt to assert the great principle of the responsibility of all agents of the Executive to the laws.' 'This great public duty may be discharged without the help of the Government: without the help of the people it cannot. It is their cause; and we will not be wanting to them, if they are not wanting to us.'

During the course of the long debate, there were hurried conferences on the floor of the House between Adderley, the Attorney General, and Disraeli. When Adderley had moved the rejection of all four of Buxton's resolutions, the Conservative Government had found itself in an uncomfortable position. After all, an impartial Royal Commission had already determined that there *had* been excessive punishment in Jamaica. Could Her Majesty's Government be placed in the position of bringing into question the integrity of Her Majesty's Commissioners? Furthermore, a vote against the first resolution would place the Tories in the hard role of a party without feelings. But would the Tory party be doing harm to Governor Eyre should it subscribe to the first resolution? On the contrary, as the Attorney General had explained to Disraeli, the use of the word 'punishment' in the resolution bestowed upon the Jamaica proceedings creates an aura of legality, and not even the warmest defender of the Governor ought to be disturbed at this affixing of a parliamentary seal of legality.

Disraeli then rose in the Chamber to propose a compromise: he promised Tory support of the first resolution if Buxton would withdraw the other three. In passing the first resolution, the House would only express what the words expressed, and not the interpretation placed upon them by Buxton. Indeed, the Chancellor added, 'I must protest against that interpretation.' Of course, there was no one in the House that did not deplore what had taken place in Jamaica, but, as the resolution assumed, everything done in Jamaica had been done legally. The supporters of the Governor were further asked to note that the passing of the resolution would not bind the Government to act against individuals. Its passage, in fact, would settle the matter entirely, so far as the Government was concerned.

The resolution was put;

> That this House deplores the excessive punishments which followed the suppression of the disturbances of October last in the parish of St Thomas, Jamaica, and especially the unnecessary frequency with which the punishment of death was inflicted,

and was unanimously agreed to.

Both Tory and Whig leaders hoped that the Jamaica Committee agitation had been dealt its *coup de grâce*. Buxton, happy in triumph, agreed to withdraw his three remaining resolutions, after obtaining assurances that they would receive the attention of the Government departments responsible. The House turned to other business—relieved that the unpleasantness was over. But the unpleasantness had only begun. The Jamaica Committee was far from being satisfied—and Eyre's homecoming was to set off a new chain of controversy.

A few days after the debate in the Commons, on 2nd August 1866, the Earl of Carnarvon, the Secretary of State for Colonies, spoke concerning Governor Eyre in the House of Lords. 'Promptitude, courage, fearlessness of responsibility, if not accompanied by a sound judgment on the part of the person who possesses them,' he declared, 'become faults rather than virtues.' Indeed, Carnarvon continued, 'the first attribute demanded of a Governor is not only justice but perfect impartiality and the power of rising above panic and the apprehensions of the moment.' 'It is to the fatal want of this quality in Mr Eyre that we may trace at least half of the mischief which arose after the outbreak.' This verdict of the Tory colonial minister, one of a chronic impulsiveness and a lack of good judgment, was severe, but more just than the view of Eyre's friends that he was a blameless hero, or that of his enemies that he was a bestial murderer. Nor was Eyre, as Forster had suggested, acting solely on racial grounds: Eyre had proved in Australia that he possessed some sympathy for the downtrodden black man. In Jamaica, he had demonstrated that he was no more ready to countenance Gordon's claims on behalf of the freedmen settlers of the hill country, than many of the English middle classes would accept Bright's claim for the right of the English working-classes to the franchise.

4

'REFORM,'
SOUTHAMPTON, AND
CHARLES KINGSLEY

The threats of the Jamaica Committee to prosecute Eyre
for murder had made many otherwise disposed people
sympathetic towards the ex-Governor. It placed them in
the awkward position of having to justify the Jamaica
excesses, in order to be fair to the 'persecuted man.' Other
incidents of June and July 1866 were leading an even
wider segment of people to a wholehearted approval of
Eyre's conduct in Jamaica. The public, indeed, was coming more and more to believe that the Governor had
handled the 'black rabble' of Jamaica admirably. What
gave rise to this feeling were the new tactics of the Reform
strategists. Not since the Chartist agitation of the 'thirties
and 'forties had there been such political activity on the
part of British workingmen. What was at issue was the
suffrage. Working-class leaders had organized a Reform
League to fight for extension of the suffrage and they
were supported in the struggle by the Radical M.P.'s like
Bright, Mill, and Hughes. When the Russell government
resigned to make way for the Conservatives, the fight for
the vote was translated from the halls of parliament to the
streets and squares of the kingdom. Unsuccessful in 'per-
suasion,' the Reformers were to attempt intimidation.
They were determined to use the threat of revolution to
obtain electoral reform.

It was shortly after the resignation of the Liberal
Government that the first great Reform demonstration was

held. On the 29th of June, about 10,000 'respectable
artisans'—in the phrase of the newspaper reports—had met
in Trafalgar Square to protest against the resignation of the
Russell government. The square was crowded, and even
the terrace in front of the National Gallery was filled with
cheering spectators. Brass-bands played noisily. Two giant
red flags flew over the assemblage: on one was emblazoned
the Liberty Cap of the French Revolution and on the
other the simple motto 'Reform.' After several speakers
had denounced the Tories and praised Reform, the crowd
unanimously approved by shouts and applause a resolution which viewed with alarm 'the advent of the Tories
to power, as being destructive to freedom at home and
favourable to despotism abroad,' and the meeting ad-
journed. But the high spirits of the crowd craved further
action. About 7,000 of the workingmen marched off to the
house of William Gladstone, the former Liberal Chancellor
of the Exchequer, who had been the strongest cabinet
supporter of Reform. When they arrived at his home at
Carlton Gardens, they cheered lustily and called for
Gladstone. Finally a servant came to the door to tell them
that the statesman was not at home. The crowd then
called for Mrs Gladstone. After a few minutes, Mrs Gladstone and her two daughters came to the balcony, pale but
smiling. The mob cheered, clapped their hands, and cried
'Gladstone for ever.' The ladies waved and hurriedly
returned within. From Gladstone's house, the crowd went
on to Pall Mall, stood in front of the Reform Club, and
cheered some more. Some Liberal members of parliament
who were at the Club at the time came out and spoke
to the workingmen. Now, tired of cheering the friends of
Reform, the crowd turned its attention to the Carlton
Club, the Tory stronghold. Hoots and groans and cries of
'Down with the Tories,' and 'Down with Lord Derby' were
kept up for about half-an-hour. The gentlemen of the
Carlton Club were concerned about the possibility of
violence, but none occurred. Finally, there was a cry of
'Home' which most of the crowd, exhausted after their
evening of shouting, obeyed. A competing cry of 'To Lord
Elcho's,' however, was heeded by some 500. Lord Elcho

was a leader of the fight against Reform and, as noted, one of Governor Eyre's earliest defenders. When these workingmen arrived at St. James Street where Elcho's house was situated, they found the police blocking their way. They were in no mood for trouble, and after giving three groans for his lordship, the crowd dispersed. By eleven o'clock, peace reigned again in fashionable London.

Although noisy and a trifle rowdy, this first demonstration was harmless enough. Yet it caused some concern to British respectability which felt that a mob, once assembled, was capable of anything. Although the 'respectable' classes felt ties of consanguinity, on the whole they regarded the London rabble much as the thirteen thousand whites of Jamaica regarded the 400,000 blacks. Like the Negro, the white rabble was tainted from birth and irredeemable, their unhappy condition an inevitable result of laziness, drunkenness, and want of thrift. And, like the whites of Jamaica, the 'respectable' classes felt themselves a small and exposed and fearful minority.

These fears became acute a month later when a demonstration called by the Reform League at Hyde Park had the feel and smell of revolution. A giant Reform demonstration had been scheduled on 23rd July 1866, but the authorities—taking fright—had decided to close the park. The Government lined policemen—on foot and mounted—before all park entrances to prevent crowds from entering. The Reform League leadership was anxious to avoid violence and was determined to keep their Frankenstein in check, while at the same time securing the greatest political benefit from its use. The League proposed to march to the park, to demand the right to enter, but, if refused, to withdraw and hold its meeting at Trafalgar Square. At the appointed hour, files of workingmen, led by fife and drum bands, marched to Hyde Park. A body of between 1,600 and 1,800 policemen was posted at the gates. A committee of the League, headed by Beales himself, marched up to the police guards and demanded the right to enter. The police refused. Beales turned to the great crowd and urged the demonstrators to follow him to Trafalgar Square, where they would hold their meeting.

Only a few workingmen followed Beales, however. The mob was determined to storm the gates of Hyde Park.

In solid phalanx, the mob marched upon the police at the entrances. The police-horses shied, lifted their hooves in the air, frequently bringing them down upon the line of workingmen. The mob began to push over the railings which barred its way. The policemen were free with their truncheons, injuring many, some of whom had later to be hospitalized. Some Reform League leaders who tried to persuade the crowd to desist and to follow Beales to Trafalgar Square were called police-spies for their pains. A company of Grenadier Guards and a troop of Life Guards came on the scene to join the police in defending the park. But it was too late; many breaches of the police line and of the railings had been effected and small groups of workingmen swarmed into the park at various points, held small meetings, and passed resolutions. The peaceful tones of the resolutions appeared to belie the act of violent opposition to authority. As the late darkness of the summer night fell, the crowd thinned. By ten o'clock, only a few persons remained within the park.

But the July sun which had in the previous century showered its warm blessings upon two great revolutions might have added a third to its rolls. Long into the night of July 23rd the executive council of the Reform League deliberated further action. The workingmen members of the executive council were exasperated by the brutal treatment meted out by the police. They determined to return to Hyde Park—and soon—and this time they would come *armed*. Beales remonstrated with his fellow council members, warned them of the consequences of their action. The fiery debate continued for several days. The Government, having got wind of what was happening, made military preparations to resist any attempt to 'take' Hyde Park by force. John Stuart Mill—known to the workingmen as a friend of Reform—came, at the invitation of the Council, to join in the debate, along with several other Radical M.P.'s. It was Mill's arguments in favour of restraint which won over the extremists. 'I told them,' Mill later wrote, 'that a proceeding which would certainly

produce a collision with the military, could only be
justifiable on two conditions: if the position of affairs had
become such that a revolution was desirable, and if they
thought themselves able to accomplish one.' The workingmen members of the Council recognized the practical
soundness of the argument and the middle-class Radical
leaders of Reform—Beales, Bright, Mill, Hughes—breathed
sighs of relief. When the Tory Home Secretary, Sir Spencer
Walpole was informed that the Reform League would not
order the men to march against Hyde Park, he burst into
tears of gratitude.

On August 8th, a meeting at the Guildhall, with the
Lord Mayor of London presiding, was called by the Reform League and the London Workingmen's Association.
Edmond Beales described the scene at Hyde Park to those
at the meeting, painting a frightening picture of policemen
with uplifted truncheons and of the attempts to place
workingmen under the pressure of horses' hooves. 'The
prohibition of the League meeting on the 23rd of July,'
Beales concluded, 'and the exclusion of the public from
Hyde Park on that day, have done far more than a hundred such meetings could have done to advance the cause
of Reform and unite the people in its support.' What
Beales had failed to note was that the Hyde Park incident
and its stormy aftermath had also unified English respectability, had revived its fears of the workingman mob,
and had provoked a great reaction in favour of those who
—like Governor Eyre—were determined to use any means
to maintain order. Among the propertied classes, a genuine
fear of violent revolution was growing. When one examined
the political canvas, one saw that the leadership of the
suffrage fight—Bright, Beales, Hughes, Mill—and the
leadership of the Jamaica Committee was the same. What
could be more natural than to identify the two causes? It
was a thing easily done since the underlying principle of
both was identical. As the middle and upper classes
watched the mobs of shouting workingmen, their fears
naturally increased—and as their fears increased, so did
their sympathies for the recently dismissed Governor Eyre.

After the report of the Royal Commission had been made
public in April, Colonel Hobbs had been ordered to return
home to England. The Colonel's mind appeared to have
been seriously affected by the inquiry into his conduct.
He had been especially disturbed by the inquiry board's
view that he had been more severe and cruel in putting
down the insurrection than he need have been. An old
soldier, Hobbs had served valiantly at the siege of
Sebastopol during the Crimean War. Never before had
his actions, performed in the line of duty, in obedience to
the orders of his superiors, been questioned. First he sulked
silently in his quarters; then he muttered his protests at
the injustices done him; then he ranted, and quite wildly.
His increasingly strange behaviour led to his being examined by a board of medical officers. The board reluctantly declared the Colonel of unsound mind.

In May of 1866, Hobbs, his wife and their three
children had been put on board the inter-colonial packet,
Tyne, on the first leg of their journey homeward. Hobbs
was placed in the hands of an army surgeon during the
voyage and two orderlies were assigned to watch him.
At no time was he to be left without at least one of his
guards—those had been the orders given by the Kingston
medical authorities. On 9th May 1866, the second day
after leaving Jamaica, when the *Tyne* was off the coast of
Haiti, Hobbs somehow managed to elude the orderly and
threw himself off one of the main-deck ports. The call of
man overboard was raised and the *Tyne* stopped in mid-
sea. A small boat was lowered to search for the Colonel
amid the waves but with no success. Some of the passengers who had observed the incident reported that Hobbs
had made no effort to save himself—had simply allowed
himself to be swallowed by the waves. After laying-to for
some time, the ship started up again, bearing a grieving
widow and three crying children back to England, where
the enemies of Governor Eyre were to insist that Hobbs
had been hounded to suicide by his conscience, and his
friends to blame the persecution of Exeter Hall. But little
was said of Colonel Hobbs' homecoming tragedy. All eyes

were on Governor, now ex-Governor, Eyre—who, too, would soon be coming home.

Eyre had been relieved of his post as Governor of Jamaica and had been severely criticized for his excessive severity in suppressing the insurrection. This had been a bitter pill. He was not a rich man—he and his family were entirely dependent upon the salary he earned. Now, not only was that to be taken from him, but he was also reprimanded, publicly disgraced. Furthermore, he had been informed that a Committee had been formed in England whose intention it was to prosecute him for murder. It must have been with some anxiety that Eyre prepared to sail for England in mid-summer of 1866.

On 24th July 1866, the day following the Hyde Park riot in London, Eyre and his family piled into the handsome gubernatorial carriage and set off for the Royal Mail Steam Company's wharf at Kingston to board the boat which was to take them back. If he was returning to a hostile England, he was leaving a Kingston which regarded him as hero and saviour. All along his way people cheered from their windows, and waved their handkerchiefs from the roadside. At the wharf, there were throngs of people who had come to wave farewell. They shouted their blessings upon the Governor and his family and wished them a good voyage and a happy return. A military band played 'God Save the Queen' as Eyre boarded the ship. On board, the ex-Governor of Jamaica found a committee representing 1,200 signers to an address which was, then, presented to him. The address rejoiced that the Royal Commission had praised Eyre's 'skill, promptitude, and vigour' in suppressing the rebellion and expressed sympathy with Eyre on those issues in which the Commission had found him sadly wanting. The Committee was composed of the leading planters and merchants of the island and their tribute brought tears to the Governor's eyes.

Eyre replied that it was only natural after so many years of service that 'I should feel some pain and regret that my career should now be abruptly terminated by removal from the public service under the disapproval and censure of the Colonial Minister.' Eyre then asserted that the execution of Gordon had had 'more effect in preventing further risings' than any other government action, and his listeners nodded sincere agreement. He bid Jamaica a reluctant farewell. 'I now retire into private life, dismissed from the public service, after nearly a lifetime spent in it; but I have at least the consolation of feeling that there has been nothing in my conduct to merit it, nothing to occasion self-reproach, nothing to regret.' Before taking final leave of the island, Eyre was presented with still another address, this one from the bishop and clergy of Kingston who thanked him for 'the lively and discriminating interest which you have ever manifested and exercised for the welfare of the church.'

A Jamaican newspaper described the harbour ceremonies during the ex-Governor's leave taking:

> The British ensign at the Royal Mail Company's Wharf was dipped three times on the arrival of his Excellency: the flags at the French and other Consulates were hoisted; and the shipping in harbour dipped three times as the noble vessel passed each of them with the ill-used but faithful and true servant of the British Crown, and the heroic and valiant rescuer of the well-disposed and peaceable and loyal inhabitants of poor Jamaica.

Certainly this was a more kindly view of the Governor than the press had taken some two years earlier. When the Governor's boat reached Port Royal on the first leg of the journey, a seventeen-gun salute was fired, and once again a band was on hand to play first 'God Save the Queen,' and then 'Home Sweet Home,' a melody which must have occasioned some bitter thoughts on the part of the Eyre family.

The journey at sea was uneventful. On Sunday, the twelfth of August, the ex-Governor of Jamaica arrived at the bustling city port of Southampton. Upon his arrival, a committee of gentlemen of Southampton sought an interview with him and told him of plans to arrange a banquet in his honour. Happy—and rather surprised—to be greeted this pleasantly, Eyre gladly agreed to remain for the dinner scheduled for the evening of Tuesday, August 21st. Almost immediately, the pro-Eyre committee of Southampton drew up and began to circulate an address to be signed by the citizens of that town and presented to the ex-Governor at the dinner. Many hundreds of citizens affixed their signatures, during the week that followed, to the memorial welcoming Eyre back to his native land and expressing sympathy with him 'after the severe and trying circumstances by which you have been so long surrounded.'

'We, in common with a large portion of your fellow-countrymen,' the address read, 'are impressed with the conviction that by your firmness and determination, joined to that prompt action which alone makes a man in authority equal to the occasion, you saved an important British colony, protected the lives and property of the loyal colonists, and saved Jamaica from an ordeal, the memory of which no time would have effaced.' They regretted that Eyre had been 'sacrificed to circumstances, as many a great man has been before,' and assured him that his fellow-countrymen appreciated and honoured him and looked forward to his return to public life. 'We rejoice,' the address concluded, 'to be the first to welcome you with this testimony of public opinion, to offer a respectful and warm-hearted welcome to Mrs Eyre and to your children, expressing an anxious and earnest hope that once more in England with your family and your friends you may speedily be restored to the blessings of health, and be cheered by the assurance of the respect, the attachment, and the confidence of all classes of your fellow-countrymen.'

It was soon clear that 'all classes' of Englishmen did not agree with the sentiments of the framers of the address. Many citizens of Southampton—workingmen and middle-class Radicals—keenly disapproved of Eyre's being fêted in their city and arranged a public meeting on the very evening of the forthcoming dinner for the purpose, as a placard announcing the meeting stated, 'of condemning the wholesale hanging, shooting, and flogging that followed the suppression of the outbreak in Jamaica, and also to protest against the ill-advised attempts of a few persons in this town to connect the people of Southampton with a demonstration in favour of ex-Governor Eyre, who has been censured and recalled by the Government for his conduct in relation to these deplorable events.' A deputation from the Jamaica Committee in London was invited— and agreed to attend—this public meeting at the Victoria Rooms, Southampton. The anti-Eyre group began to tack posters all over the city, announcing their own meeting and proclaiming the disgrace of Southampton by 'the feast of blood,' their description of the dinner to be given for Eyre. 'The very stones of Southampton would cry murder,' one placard read. On the day before the scheduled dinner, a particularly vituperative handbill bearing the Royal coat-of-arms reversed and headed 'Banquet of Death' was widely distributed all over Southampton by a workingmen's group. This handbill was immediately disavowed by the citizens who had called the Victoria Rooms meeting.

When the evening of the dinner arrived, a distinguished group of men had come to do Eyre honour. The diners included the Earl of Cardigan, the famous commander of the Light Brigade during the Crimean War; the Earl of Shrewsbury and Talbott; the Earl of Hardwicke; and the noted poet, novelist, and historian, the Reverend Charles Kingsley. All the gentlemen present—about one hundred of them—were introduced to the guest of honour; the Mayor of Southampton welcomed Eyre to his city in the most complimentary terms; and a leading member of the committee which had arranged the dinner read aloud the circulated address which at this point bore the signatures of about 1,000 of Southampton's citizens. Edward Eyre rose to respond to the testimonial of Southampton's confidence in him in a speech, his first in England, which was to be his most complete public defence of his conduct. It was a brief address which revealed him as capable of an intelligent—and even a sensitive—presentation of his position:

I feel deeply touched by your generous and friendly address, welcoming me to England on my return from a most harassing and anxious service in Jamaica. It is most gratifying to me to find that, notwithstanding all the unfavourable opinions which have been expressed of the action which I found it necessary to take under a very great emergency, you recognize in that action the means which protected the lives and properties of the colonists and saved an important colony to the Crown. With you I sincerely deplore that some excesses occurred during the continuance of martial law, but such must always be more or less unavoidable under that condition, and especially when a great extent of country of such a character as that of Jamaica is occupied by a mere handful of troops amid a numerous and disaffected peasantry. Had any less prompt or less decisive measures been adopted than those which martial law affords it is certain that the rebellion would rapidly have extended, and in the long run there would have been a far greater sacrifice of human life, a larger destruction of property, and a vastly increased amount of suffering and misery. Severity in such a case appeared to me to be in reality true mercy.

At the same time I can respect the opinion of those who, in sincerity and from good impulses, believe that this severity was continued for a longer period than was necessary as a measure of self-preservation. To them I would say that, while they possess much information with regard to the details of the proceedings under martial law which was not before me at the time, they are unable to realize the fearful responsibility which I felt would attach to me had I interfered to stay summary trials by court martial too soon, and thereby removed that dread of immediate and severe retribution which undoubtedly prevented rebellion from breaking out in other parts of the island. . . .

For the expression of unabated confidence in my integrity and honour I am deeply indebted to you. It is most cheering to me to know that you appreciate the spirit by which I was actuated, and that you believe

that in all I did my single desire was to do my duty
faithfully as a servant of the Crown. I value very highly
the sympathy which you extend to me on my return,
under somewhat trying circumstances, to a country
which I have served to the best of my knowledge and
ability, and I will allow myself to say, with all my heart
and with all my strength. . . .

Governor Eyre sat down to the prolonged applause and
cheers of the dinner guests. His speech had been dignified,
with no boastful shouts about the brutal business—such as
had come from the lips of many of his English supporters
in their clubs, in the privacy of their drawing rooms, at
their tables over brandy, who spoke not of 'unavoidable'
necessity but rather of 'serves the blackguards quite right.'
The first of the after-dinner speakers, the Earl of Cardigan,
was cast in this mould. The Radicals would have regarded
the seventh Earl of Cardigan as a most appropriate
speaker at a 'Banquet of Blood.' Cruel and arrogant,
Cardigan had gained a reputation as a flogger of troopers
and had subjected his subordinate officers to such indig-
nities that at one time the War Office had been compelled
to request his resignation. His conduct had become a
national scandal, and, in the early 'forties, he had been
one of the most unpopular men in England, jeered at
whenever recognized. Public meetings were held, at that
time, to petition the Queen for his dismissal from the
service. He had become a chief target of the parliamentary Radical leaders of the 'forties, humanitarians who
campaigned steadfastly against flogging in the services.
His reputation had been somewhat rehabilitated by his
heroism at Balaclava, but his character as a flogger of
troopers was not forgotten. Now, at Southampton, Cardigan had come to praise not Eyre as he had been depicted
by Cardwell or Forster, but Eyre as the flogger of Jamaica
Negroes. How could the picture of Eyre painted by the
Governor's most severe enemies fail to appeal to Cardigan?
The Earl's speech was brief. He spoke of two other
colonial insurrections after which allegations had been
made about 'supposed' cruelties committed in suppressing

the insurrection. 'The Prime Minister of the day stood by the governors he employed,' the Tory Earl asserted amid shouts of approval. 'Such Prime Ministers and such men were Lord Palmerston and his predecessor, Lord Melbourne.' 'In those days,' Cardigan continued, 'the Imperial Government stood by their governors and carried their case through Parliament. No governor, no matter what might be the cruelties—if they were cruelties—necessarily committed on those occasions was ever seriously found fault with; no governor placed in such a position ever was injured for life.' Another speaker, Lord Shrewsbury, spoke as a Jamaica property owner, who, as he asserted, knew full well that Eyre had saved that colony for the Queen. Shrewsbury gave his support to Eyre 'regardless of what might be said of him by a faction who pretended to more humanity than fell to the lot of human nature' and who 'combined political with religious dissent.' He was ashamed that the government was so much under the thumb of John Bright as not to stand by its officer. Lord Hardwicke, a landowner of the Southampton district, described the Jamaica insurrection as one of 'free people who enjoyed all the liberties we do; of a people who enjoy much more happiness and much more wealth than fall to the lot of the labouring population of England.' It was an insurrection, Hardwicke continued, of 'thousands against hundreds. Those who rose were a half-educated—I might almost say an uncivilized people.' 'If your house be on fire, will you complain of the fireman who in flooding the flames destroys the incendiary by drowning him?'

Sharing with Cardigan the distinction of being the speaker best known to the public, was the Reverend Charles Kingsley, the poet and novelist, and at that time Regius Professor of Modern History at Cambridge. In the late 'forties, the young clergyman had become a disciple of the Christian Socialism of F. D. Maurice, and in the early 'fifties, he had written two social novels in which the hard life of the working class and the rapacity of the sweater and the landlord were tellingly depicted. Needless to add, he had at that time been regarded with marked coolness by church, and court, and peerage. But his subsequent

writings had made him a favourite in these circles. This
new Kingsley, patriotic and martial, had written, during
the Crimean War, a stirring pamphlet, *Brave Words for
Brave Soldiers*, which had been widely distributed to the
Army, and in the course of that struggle had observed to
a friend that the taking of life in battle was 'the strongest
assertion of the dignity and divineness of national life.' In
1855, his *Westward Ho!*, a highly patriotic historical novel
about Elizabethan buccaneers, brought him court attention and favour, and, later, appointment, as one of
Victoria's chaplains-in-ordinary, and, in 1860, as Regius
Professor of Modern History at Cambridge.

Kingsley entered the Eyre controversy at Southampton
almost by accident. During the summer of 1866, he had
been the house guest of Lord Hardwicke at Sidney Lodge,
that nobleman's country estate. When the Eyre banquet
was being arranged, Hardwicke had determined to attend
and had asked his guest to join him. In his speech, the
Regius professor confessed his ignorance of the details of
the Jamaica insurrection, but, he related, his brother,
Henry, had written an article on Eyre's Australian explorations and much admired the ex-Governor. Therefore
he would take Governor Eyre and all his actions in Jamaica
'upon trust.' Eyre represented the 'English spirit of in-
domitable perseverance, courage, and adventure' and of
'good nature, of temper, of the understanding of human
beings, of knowing how to manage men.' His activities in
Australia had showed that he had 'in a very high degree
that English spirit which had carried the Anglo-Saxon
tongue round the world and had made us the fathers of
the United States and the conquerors of India.' Kingsley
ventured to prophesy that Eyre, since he was so much the
embodiment of the English spirit, would, in all likelihood,
be given a peerage. In uttering this, the poet-clergyman
contrived his own undoing. Perhaps he had chosen what
he was about to say as a graceful compliment to his host,
Lord Hardwicke, but it was later regarded, in the words
of a Liberal review, as an 'explosion of flunkeyism'; 'such
a speech,' the journal was to add, 'is one of those surprises

which provoke only a faintly amused laughter; it is like a
bad pun, mirthful because of an absurd incongruity.'

> Mr Eyre [said Kingsley] is so noble, brave, and
> chivalric a man, so undaunted a servant of the Crown,
> so illustrious as an explorer in Australia and a saviour of
> society in the West Indies, that Peers—actually Peers
> —my soul sinks with awe as I repeat *Peers*—members of
> the 'sacred' order, which represents chivalry, which
> adopts into its ranks all genius, all talents, all virtue,
> and all beauty, condescend, not indeed to give him a
> dinner—that would be too much—but to dine in the same
> room with him.

This paragraph supplied useful ammunition for the Governor's enemies.

At the close of the evening, Eyre thanked the dinner
guests for relieving his apprehensions as to how he would
be received in England. He had only tried to do his duty,
he declared. 'From my heart, gentlemen, I thank you one
and all for the cordial welcome you have given to me.' It
was especially gratifying, he said, lifting his head up to the
galleries, where the ladies sat, to be welcomed at such a
banquet 'graced as it is by the presence of so many of the
fair, the gentle, and the good'; those, indeed, 'never would
have cheered me with their countenances on this occasion
if they thought I could be capable of the cruelty and
injustice which some persons attribute to me.' The ladies
cheered, cordially surrounded Mrs Eyre and the children,
and applauded them. Several more toasts were drunk, and,
finally, the assembled company—in the very gayest of
spirits after so much wine—rose from the table, and began
to file out of the Hall into the hot August evening.

The first of the diners to arrive at the entrance to the
Philharmonic Hall was greeted by a surprising sight. High
Street was thronged by a howling mob. The street which
had been so peacefully empty when the guests had arrived
for their dinner was now crowded by men and women who
noisily hooted as each carriage drove up to receive its
owner. It was a crowd of 'roughs,' in the parlance of the

day, coarse bruisers who made up the van of city mobs, spoiling for a fight, heedless of the claims of order and decency. Some of the crowd demanded that Eyre—that 'blood-thirsty tyrant'—be handed over to them and seemed fully prepared to lynch him on the spot. Others satisfied themselves by hurling less genteel epithets at the former Governor. The diners clapped their hands and cheered loudly so as to drown out the abuse. But this only infuriated the mob further. As each carriage drove off, there was a violent rush upon it. Crowds of men and women surrounded many carriages and forced open their doors to see if Eyre were inside. The gentlemen, of course, did all they could to push the intruders off and the coachmen vigorously forced their horses through the onrushing people. Many persons were thrown down; others were run over by the carriages. Women in the crowd screamed in terror.

While this street demonstration of 'roughs' was taking place on High Street, outside the Philharmonic Hall, a heavily attended meeting of the 'respectable' working class of Southampton was still in session at the Victoria Rooms. On the following morning, Southampton newspapers reported that this assemblage had constituted the largest working-class meeting that the city of Southampton had ever known. The workingmen who attended adopted resolutions protesting against the defence of Eyre by the local gentry and aristocracy and the 'disgrace' brought 'upon the British name' and upon the city of Southampton by the dinner held in Eyre's honour.

The following day, the news of the happenings at Southampton—the dinner, the speeches, the mob scene, the meeting of protest—was being read and discussed at dinner tables throughout the country. The violence of the High Street mob served only to reinforce the identification of the Jamaica affair with the previous month's reform riots. With the Governor's return, the controversy had entered a new and more violent phase.

In early 1868, nearly two years after the banquet of August 1866, the London *Times* was to refer to it as 'the

absurd demonstration in honour of Mr Eyre at Southampton.' If the banquet were absurd—and the heaping of
bouquets upon a governor ignominiously removed from
office and gravely censured for faulty judgment may indeed be so regarded—why did *The Times*, which had
ceased to worship at the Governor's image after the
publication of the Royal Commission report, fail to call
attention to this absurdity in 1866? Why did not public
opinion—the bulk of the articulate middle classes—denounce
the Southampton banquet? We have already noted the
answer: *The Times*—in agreement with the 'public'—did not
wish to join in the Jamaica Committee's 'persecution,' and,
after the Hyde Park affair, the public was not at all certain
if Eyre's conduct in Jamaica were not, after all, the only
way to handle a rabble gone mad. Therefore, *The Times*
—like the bulk of the English middle-classes—maintained
a discreet, sympathetic silence, if not a wholly approving
one. But to the members of the Jamaica Committee, and to
the Radical press, this silence bespoke unqualified approval
of Eyre's conduct. Eyre's friends had called for the
emulation of their hero. Was this not a highly dangerous
example? The fêting of Eyre at Southampton reinforced
the determination of the Jamaica Committee not to be
satisfied with the Governor's dismissal nor with a highly
general parliamentary resolution deploring 'excesses.' They
were now certain that Eyre had to be tried for his crimes
by a court of law.

The Southampton display also re-activated the London
working-class, which had made no dramatic moves since
the reform riot of the previous month. It was on Thursday,
the 30th of August, that a public open-air meeting,
provoked by reports of the Southampton dinner, was held
at Bartholomew Close, London. The principal speaker, a
workingman named James Finlan, discussed Charles Kingsley's address and agreed with the writer-clergyman that
Eyre should be made a peer, for in the House of Lords,
Finlan asserted, the 'wholesale murderer' would find kindred souls, and his beastly virtues would be fully appreciated. Finlan urged the workers to support the efforts
of the Jamaica Committee. A second speaker neatly

packaged the Jamaica events and the Reform agitation
into one parcel: a Tory government had as much right to
shoot down people in Hyde Park as Mr Eyre had to
murder hundreds of innocent Jamaicans. The House of
Lords was roundly denounced by speaker after speaker
both for its opposition to Reform and for its representation
among the Southampton diners. The aristocracy as a body,
one speaker asserted, was everywhere opposed to the
rights of the people and was always ready to support
bloody oppression. Another speaker found it amazing that
ladies could have been present at the banquet. One could
expect almost anything from earls but he rather expected
better of 'respectable English ladies.' The meeting concluded with the passing of a resolution pledging the workingmen 'to support the Jamaica Committee in its endeavour
to remove the stain the conduct of ex-Governor Eyre has
cast upon the fame of Great Britain.'

This Thursday meeting was simply a preliminary to a
more important event scheduled for the following Monday
evening, September 3rd. A great crowd was assembled
at Clerkenwell Green under the auspices of the group of
workingmen who had called the Bartholomew Close meeting. The crowd had come together in response to a placard
which was headed, in huge capital letters,

'THE MONSTER, EX-GOVERNOR EYRE'

and went on to announce that 'this wholesale murderer
will be tried by a jury of 10,000 workingmen at a torch-
light meeting on Clerkenwell Green, Monday evening,
September 3rd, and if found guilty will be burnt in effigy
on a gallows, with our wishes that we should like to serve
him and his aristocratic retainers in the same manner in
the flesh. The judge will take the chair in front of the
sessions-house at 7 o'clock. By order of the great meeting
held in Bartholomew-close.' When the meeting began, the
effigy—a most carefully constructed dummy of the Governor—was in its place ready for the burning, an event
which was to climax the evening's proceedings. The meeting had hardly got underway, however, when the dummy

began to burn through some accident. In a short while it had been entirely consumed. As a consequence, Governor Eyre was burned in effigy without benefit of trial and before his crimes had been fully denounced by the half-dozen prosecuting barristers on the platform. Nevertheless, the speeches of these 'barristers' were made, and, though seemingly futile since the purpose of the evening had already been fulfilled, they were none the less violent.

From these addresses, it soon became obvious that Eyre was to burn in effigy primarily as a symbol of 'his aristocratic abettors.' Speaker after speaker denounced these 'dwellers in ducal mansions, who never earned 2d. in their lives,' who had 'no sympathy or feeling for the toilers who made England what she is.' One of the speakers, an extremist, shouted 'We are all Republicans at heart,' but the crowd greeted this avowal in a most lukewarm manner. Whereupon, sensing the temper of his audience, he switched his views and proclaimed Victoria the best sovereign since Alfred the Great. One of the earnest workingmen in the crowd wondered aloud why the speaker had had to go back to the time of Alfred since 'that was almost two centuries ago.' The final speaker of the evening was a socialist (it should be noted that Karl Marx's First International had its headquarters in London during the period of the Jamaica affair, and that the International included the chief British trade union leaders). This socialist workingman spoke of his sympathy for his 'brother proletarians,' black or white, all over the world, and he delivered his speech with such a wealth of movement and gesticulation, and with such large expenditures of energy, that two men had to keep constant hold of his legs to prevent his toppling over from the platform into the crowd.

The platform was crowded. The leaders of the meeting and demonstration had been joined by some of the more aggressive workingmen from below the platform. They solemnly sat 'in judgement' and unanimously decided to consign Governor Eyre, or his effigy at any rate, to the flames. But, as noted, accident had already provided that fate for the mass of cloth and straw which represented the

Governor. The crowd nonetheless cheered the verdict and went home without any further displays of pyrotechnics.

The Radical newspapers of London and Manchester had been aroused to high anger by the news of the South-ampton banquet. All the diners were savagely denounced. The aristocracy was attacked for supporting irresponsible authority against justice and for desiring to employ the same tactics against British workingmen as Eyre had used against the Jamaican peasantry. Rather than be fêted, the ex-Governor ought to be caged in the Zoo and be spat upon by passers-by![1]

But the chief target of the Radical press in the days following Southampton was not the aristocracy, nor even Eyre. It was Charles Kingsley. The Radicals sensed be-trayal in Kingsley's participation in the Southampton events. He who in days past had defended the workingman had deserted—and to him was meted out the bitter fare reserved for traitors. One paper pointed out that, on his mother's side, Kingsley stemmed from West Indian planter stock, and suggested that this might account for his de-fection; another attributed his conduct to his brother Henry's enthusiastic interest in Eyre's Australian explora-tions. A weekly accused him of toadyism, of seeking fa-vour from those in the country who had it to give.

---

[1] This 'homecoming' was pictured in a handbill with which London was well-placarded after Eyre's return. It read:

As for those who incited the pirates and seamen to commit abominations laid to their charge, we must ferret them out. They must be brought down to trial. If guilty, their names shall be handed down to everlasting infamy; they shall be branded as the first murderer, Cain; they shall hang as high as Haman; or better still, be caged side by side with the wild beasts in the Zoological Gardens, so that men may spit at them when they pass by. When dead, their carcasses should be thrown to the dogs, their ashes scattered to the four winds of heaven; and as for their souls, so blacked must they be, that hell itself will scarce care to receive them.

No mean malediction, this!

What Kingsley's Radical critics had failed to grasp was that the clergyman had not necessarily been swayed by family or personal considerations—that he had, in fact, acted in accordance with deep and long-held principles. What was, after all, at issue was the principle of democracy, and Kingsley, like F. D. Maurice, the founder of Christian socialism, had never been a democrat. His political ties were with the Tories and his political goal, much like that of Disraeli, was to unite the Established Church, the aristocracy, and the workingmen against the middle-class dissenters, shop-keepers, and manufacturers. Although feeling sympathy for the poor condition of the workingman, Kingsley had no desire to admit them to a share in government. On the contrary, he considered the workingman, along with the Jamaican black, and the Irish, as 'quite unfit for self-government.' In a letter written later in 1866 to an Edinburgh professor, Kingsley took issue with John Stuart Mill's denial of congenital individual and racial superiority: 'It is this mistake,' he wrote, 'which has led him and others into that theory that the suffrage ought to be educational and formative.' 'Society may pity those who are born fools or knaves, but she cannot, for her own sake, allow them power if she can help it,' Kingsley concluded. As for himself, he had *always* admired the strong and the ruthless ruler, like Rajah Brooke.[1]

---

[1] One Radical, Sir George Otto Trevelyan, an ardent admirer of Kingsley's two social novels, *Alton Locke* and *Yeast*, penned these verses:

Let's rather speak of what was felt by us who value 'Yeast'
On learning who has led the choir at that triumphal feast
Where Hampshire's town and country joined a civic wreath
    to fling
O'er him, the great proconsul, whose renown through time
    shall ring
In deathless cadence borne along pianoforte wires,
As memories heroic haunt the choirs of Grecian lyres.

. . . . That he, who gave our ancient creeds their first and
    rudest shock,
Till half the lads for pattern took his Chartist Alton Locke,

The press criticism was very hard upon Kingsley. He was greatly disturbed at this reward for having come to Southampton to help 'a man whom I believe ill-used, calumniated, and hunted to death by fanatics,' as he wrote to a friend. For such manifestly good intentions, 'men insult me.' 'I have been cursed for it, as if I had been a dog, who had never stood for the workingman when all the world was hounding him down in 1848-49, and imperilled my own prospects in life on behalf of freedom and justice.' Having been the first to expose himself to Radical fire, and been badly seared, Kingsley hung back from taking an active part in the two years of controversy which followed Southampton. His forthright stand behind Governor Eyre in August 1866, however, broke the ties which remained between himself and his chief Christian Socialist colleagues of the days of 1848, Thomas Hughes and J. M. Ludlow, both of whom had become members of the Jamaica Committee. Kingsley's failure to follow up his stand at Southampton and to join the subsequent fight to vindicate Eyre severely impaired his relationship with two other friends—John Ruskin and Thomas Carlyle—who were to become the Governor's leading defenders in the months ahead, and who came to regard Kingsley's belated caution as cowardice.

Should tell us that Debrett within his gilded leaves contains
The virtue of the British isles, the beauty and the brains!

. . . . That he, whose brave old English tale set all our veins
     aglow,
. . . . Should teach that 'modern chivalry' has found its no-
     blest egress
In burning Baptist villages, and stringing up a negress!

5

THE GLADIATORS: CARLYLE AND
RUSKIN
V. DARWIN AND HUXLEY

About a week after the Southampton banquet, friends of
the ex-Governor began to organize a fund-raising committee to support his defence against the threatened prosecution of John Stuart Mill and his associates. At the first
meeting of the new committee, Thomas Carlyle took the
chair. Given his 'Discourse on the Nigger Question,' written over sixteen years previously, it seemed inevitable that
Carlyle would come to the aid of Governor Eyre. Was
Eyre not being attacked by the philanthropists of Exeter
Hall, by the believers in the 'rosepink sentimentality'
whom Carlyle had denounced again and again? Were not
the Reformers, the democrats, those whom Carlyle believed were bringing England to the brink of ruin, hounding the ex-Governor of Jamaica? Above all, had not
Governor Eyre behaved in the spirited, masculine fashion
of the Carlylean hero? Still, at the start of the affair, Carlyle had kept his peace. Some of his friends, indeed, believed he would keep out of the controversy. Carlyle, they
explained, was an old man and might not feel sufficiently
energetic to play an active part. Then also, others added,
it might be that Eyre's conduct in Jamaica—the ex-
Governor's defence of the flogging of women, for example
—did not quite commend itself to the heroic standard
which Carlyle had erected. But these suppositions were
not correct.

Some months before Southampton, in April, Carlyle's

wife Jane had written to her husband about a tiff she had had with a gentleman while visiting a friend in the country. There had been a lively discussion of the report of the Royal Commission. This gentleman, Jane Carlyle reported, 'would have had Eyre cut into small pieces, and eaten raw.' 'He told me *women* might patronize Eyre—that women were naturally cruel, and rather liked to look on while horrors were perpetrated. But *no* man living could stand up for Eyre now!' Jane's reply had been 'I hope Mr Carlyle does,' adding 'I haven't had an opportunity of asking him; but I should be surprised and grieved if I found him sentimentalizing over a pack of black brutes!' The gentleman stared hard at her for a moment and then said: 'Mr Carlyle! Oh, yes! Mr Carlyle! One cannot indeed swear what he will *not* say! His greatest aim and philosophy of life being "The smallest happiness of the fewest number!"'

In 1866, Carlyle was over seventy years old—the universally acclaimed dean of Victorian letters. A Scotsman, born at Ecclefechan in Annandale in 1795, he had attended village schools and had been sent to the University of Edinburgh by a father who willingly sacrificed the boy's earning power to make him a Minister of the Kirk. After years of preparation, Thomas discovered that he no longer held his former orthodox views in religious matters and began some twenty years of valiantly striving to secure a niche in the English literary world. He earned money by serving as a private tutor, by doing hack writing for encyclopedias, by translating works from the German and by writing articles for the reviews—all with little success. From this period dated his dyspepsia, which was, he once said, like a rat gnawing at the pit of his stomach.

In 1831, Carlyle had made the acquaintance of John Stuart Mill, who became one of the earliest of what was to become an army of admirers, and who thought he recognized a fellow Radical in the young Scotsman. Partly because of personal factors, but primarily because of Mill's growing awareness that Carlyle's 'radicalism' was quite different from his own, the gap between the friends widened. Their opinions became more and more opposed, and the depth of the chasm which separated them had been set before the readers of *Fraser's Magazine* in 1849, as we have seen. Although Carlyle had abandoned the stern Calvinist doctrine in which he had been reared, he still believed it a good code for the governing of social and political relations. He accepted the vocation of chastising the British people for their worship of Mammon, and condemned the materialism of his time in favour of a 'spiritual,' an 'idealistic' view of life, borrowed from Goethe and Fichte. He became the apostle of 'feeling,' of 'sentiment,' and the fierce opponent of the new industrial England of the chimney stacks. He took up the cause of the factory operatives, working under miserable conditions for low wages, and uncovered the thousand and one shams which underlay the doctrine of laissez-faire. Finally, like a latter-day Jeremiah, he warned that, unless some improvement were effected, England might find itself facing revolution. In good Calvinist fashion, Carlyle preached the gospel of work which made holy. (It had been in this spirit that he had written his discourse on the Negro question.) But if good, work was organized heartlessly under laissez-faire. Nothing bound master and men in their common undertaking but wages, the cash-nexus, and thus there could be no pride in craftsmanship, no security of employment, no provision for sickness or old age. As an alternative, Carlyle suggested that the workers be organized in industry on a military model, being hired for life on a permanent contract at a just wage—a real system, as he wrote, of 'mastership and servantship.' Carlyle's opponents saw in all this nothing but praise of slavery, which indeed, he described as preferable to 'free hire' in his discourse of 1849. He had urged first the new class of manufacturers and then, losing faith in them, the landed aristocracy, to behave like heroes and usher in the new society. Calvinism had been predicated upon the doctrine of the elect, the view that certain among us have been 'chosen' from birth to enjoy salvation while others were inevitably damned. Heroes were the earthly elect—those specially chosen to rule—and Carlyle preached the doctrine of 'hero-worship.' Frederick the Great, the final volume of whose biography Carlyle had completed in the year of the Jamaica revolt, was such a hero, in Carlyle's mind, as was Oliver Cromwell, the Puritan despot who had added Jamaica to the growing British Empire in the middle of the seventeenth century, about whom he had also written. Heroes were guided by a special morality, the morality of might which, in their hands, made right.

In 1841, Carlyle had delivered a series of lectures on heroes and hero-worship in London. Mill, at that time still the older man's friend, got up in the midst of one of Carlyle's lectures and, not being able to restrain himself, shouted 'No, no.' An embarrassed, red-faced Mill was then led from the public hall. If in 1841, Mill could still have been startled, by the 'sixties, most of Carlyle's ideas had become widely known. His views on contemporary politics were very much in line with his political philosophy. During the American Civil War, Carlyle had idealized the condition of the Negro slave in the South and supported the Confederacy. Carlyle professed not to be able to understand why people should be 'cutting throats indefinitely to put the Negro into a position for which all experience shows him unfit.' As for slavery, Carlyle regarded that as a thoroughly desirable institution.

All of Carlyle's views were at stake in the Eyre controversy: his hero-worship, his contempt for democracy, his antipathy towards the Negro, his disgust for the philanthropy of Exeter Hall and the individualism of the Radicals. When the Eyre Defence Committee had been formed in early August, the self-appointed secretary of the new committee, Alexander Hamilton Hume—an Australian living in London who, without having any idea of what had happened in Jamaica, had determined to support the man who had won fame as an explorer of his native country—immediately wrote Carlyle to ask him to lend his name to the group. The Sage of Chelsea replied to his request in a letter, dated August 23rd, which the Eyre Committee was to circulate widely:

Sir—The clamour raised against Governor Eyre appears to me to be disgraceful to the good sense of England;

and if it rested on any depth of conviction, and were
not rather (as I always flatter myself it is) a thing of rumour and hearsay, of repetition and reverberation,
mostly from the teeth outward, I should consider it of
evil omen to the country, and to its highest interests,
in these times.

For my own share, all the light that has yet reached
me on Mr Eyre and his history in the world goes steadily to establish that he is a just, humane, and valiant
man, faithful to his trusts everywhere, and with no
ordinary faculty of executing them.

. . . that penalty and clamour are not the thing this
Governor merits from any of us, but honour and
thanks. . . .

Carlyle concluded by urging a 'wise imitation' of Eyre
'should similar emergencies rise, on the great scale or on
the small, in whatever we are governing.'

Carlyle defended Eyre upon much these grounds in
private conversation. He told his good friend James An-
thony Froude, at this time the editor of *Fraser's*, that it
was 'as if a ship had been on fire; the captain, by immediate and bold exertion, had put the fire out and had been
called to account for having flung a bucket or two of water
into the hold beyond what was necessary. He had damaged some of the cargo, perhaps, but he had saved the
ship.' He keenly sympathized with the former Governor's
personal situation—recalled from office, refused other employment—in a word, ruined. A wife and several children
were dependent upon him for financial support. 'Poor
Eyre!' Carlyle wrote to a friend the day following the first
meeting of the Defence Committee, 'I am heartily sorry
for him, and for the English nation, which makes such a
dismal fool of itself.' 'Eyre, it seems,' he continued, 'has
fallen suddenly from £6,000 a year into almost zero, and
has a large family and needy kindred dependent on him.'
'Such is his reward,' Carlyle concluded, 'for saving the
West Indies, and hanging one incendiary mulatto, well
worth the gallows, if I can judge.'

Throughout his lifetime, Carlyle had condemned an-

archy which he felt proceeded from the lower, more
'brutal' classes. In 1843, for example, at the height of the
Chartist difficulties, he had urged his 'heroes' to battle
Disorder: 'Wheresoever thou findest Disorder, there is thy
eternal enemy,' he wrote. 'Attack him swiftly, subdue him;
make Order for him, the subject not of Chaos, but of
Intelligence, Divinity.' As Carlyle grew older, Disorder and
Chaos became even more real to him. An old man living
in Chelsea, he felt exposed to the taunts of street urchins,
unemployed idlers, sauntering roughs, exposed to humili-
ating insult and even to actual physical abuse. He was
infuriated that such a situation should have been possible
upon the streets of the capital, horrified that respectable
people, such as himself, should be made targets, and profoundly disturbed at his personal vulnerability. These matters were a frequent topic of his conversation. He
increasingly identified the growing agitation for Reform
with Chaos—after all, what was democracy but anarchy?
—and saw Governor Eyre as a symbol of the strong man
determined to maintain order.

An entry in Carlyle's journal for 26th September 1866,
spoke of 'Bright, Beales, Gladstone, Mill, and Co.' bringing
'on the suffrage question, kindling up the slow *canaille*
what they can. This, and "oh, make the niggers happy!"
seem to be the two things needful with these sad people.'
The inevitable result of Radical agitation, Carlyle believed,
was revolution and the destruction of all that was good in
England. 'Very questionable to me whether England won't
go quite to *smash*,' he wrote, 'perhaps better that it do,
having reached such a pitch of spiritual beggary.' In his
letter of August 23rd to Hamilton Hume, setting forth his
views on the Eyre case, Carlyle followed this reasoning:

The English nation never loved anarchy, nor was wont
to spend its sympathy on miserable mad seditions, especially of this inhuman and half-brutish type; but always loved order and the prompt suppression of
seditions, and reserved its tears for something worthier
than promoters of such delirious and fatal enterprises
who had got their wages for their sad industry. Has

the English nation changed, then, altogether? I flatter myself it has not, not yet quite; but only that certain loose superficial portions of it have become a great deal louder and not any wiser than they formerly used to be.

Although Carlyle's most active interest in the Eyre Defence Committee was limited to its first months of existence, he followed subsequent events of the controversy most carefully. Froude reported that 'I never knew him more anxious about anything.' A journalist member of the Eyre group described the Sage's behaviour at these early meetings as 'ardent, vehement, bitter.' 'Shaking his long locks as an enraged lion might have shaken his mane as he sprang upon his prey,' Carlyle addressed the meeting, 'as if in its midst had been seated his mortal foe, pouring out execrations without stint, *imagining* an opponent he was bound to crush.' 'If the negroes of Jamaica had been dealt with by this fiery man of letters' rather than by Eyre who seemed 'a merciful man' by comparison, 'events would have gone much worse for them,' the journalist concluded.

Carlyle was at first rather disappointed at the composition of the Committee. He regarded it as 'most feeble'; its secretary, Hamilton Hume, he described as a man with 'bright swift eyes' who 'showed little knowledge of his element.' The Sage was especially disappointed that Charles Kingsley was 'still hanging back afraid' after his bitter experience at the hands of the Radical press. It was necessary to attract competent and hard-working men to the cause, and Carlyle set himself this task. If the Eyre group were successful, Carlyle wrote, it would be because 'my old coat is not afraid of a little mud on the sleeve of it, as super finer ones might be.' But Carlyle was old and felt tired; he wished another to shoulder the principal burdens of the Committee. After Kingsley, Carlyle's eye alighted on his friend and disciple, the critic and writer, John Ruskin.

Ruskin's name had become a household word because of the publication of his popular *Sesame and Lilies* in 1865. In the years that followed, the noted art and literary critic was to turn more and more to criticism of the canons of political economy, the creed of the growing British capitalism. His entrance into the Eyre controversy was evidence of this interest. In December 1865, Ruskin had written a letter to the *Daily Telegraph* which had outlined his position. Ruskin had, he wrote to the paper, several months earlier, supported Hughes in his campaign for Lambeth, just as he had supported the candidacy of John Stuart Mill for Westminster, because he believed they were 'honest, thoughtful, and benevolent men.' As it happened, his views differed substantially from theirs on many important subjects, but even so, Ruskin expostulated, 'I thought better of them both than they would countenance this fatuous outcry against Governor Eyre.' There was a vital principle which separated his political views from those of Mill and Hughes. 'In most directions of thought and action,' he proclaimed, 'they are for Liberty, and I am for Lordship; they are Mob's men, and I am a King's man.' Addressing the at-that-time Liberal *Daily Telegraph,* Ruskin added: 'Yes Sir, I am one of those almost forgotten creatures, who shrivel under your daily scorn; I am a "Conservative", and hope for ever to be a Conservative in the deepest sense—a Reformer, not a Deformer.' The issue was indeed slavery; but Ruskin declared that he opposed slavery of all kinds, white as well as black, and believed that 'white emancipation not only ought to precede, but must by law of all fate precede, black emancipation.' The British workingman was a white-slave in dirty, unhealthy factories—this under the regime of the *laissez-faire* industrialism which the Radicals, the enemies of Eyre, supported. So long as this English serfdom continued to exist—and to exist, furthermore, with the blessings and approval of Messrs. Gurney and Hughes—he, Ruskin, did not intend to wax hot about the treatment of Jamaica blacks. Contrasting white and black slavery, Ruskin confessed his dislike of the 'slavery which obliges women (if it does) to carry their children over frozen rivers; but I more dislike the slavery which makes them throw their children into wells' and 'I would willingly hinder the selling of girls on the Gold Coast; but primar-

ily, if I might, would hinder the selling of them in May-
fair.' England, Ruskin concluded, could use an able
Governor like Edward Eyre. 'Let the men who would
deserve well of England' not reserve their attacks for 'those
among us who have saved colonies.'

Ruskin had thus been the first of the literary men to
come to the defence of Governor Eyre. It was even possible that the noted critic, very close to Carlyle at this
period, had helped Jane to interest her husband in the
Eyre affair. Ruskin had been coming increasingly under
the influence of Carlyle. This influence was intensified by
the death of his father which freed the son from the necessity of maintaining views opposed to the elder Ruskin's
unrelenting Toryism. High and noble goals were being
steadily subordinated to the incessant struggle for profit,
Ruskin was convinced. The lives of English workingmen
were being made nasty, short, and brutish because of
laissez-faire. For Ruskin these were the most important
political problems, in fact, the only ones worthy of consideration. In Ruskin's view, the Radicals were largely responsible for this misery. *Laissez-faire* was culpable for
the murder of thousands of British workers year in and
year out. If this were the case, was it not hypocritical for
the Radicals to bemoan so vituperatively the mote in the
eye of Governor Eyre?

Ruskin made his first appearance at the Defence Committee the week following its initial meeting. Carlyle had
asked him to come, and Ruskin, loving the old man, was
happy to take the burden of committee work off the Sage's
shoulders. He was even ready to personally subscribe
£100 to the Defence Fund. From Ruskin's diary, we
know that he had given much thought and effort to con-
structing his first speech to the Committee, on 7th September 1866. It was a speech of which he was proud, as
was Carlyle. In a letter to a friend, written a week after
its delivery, Carlyle was to speak of Ruskin's address as
'a right gallant thrust,' adding that 'while all the world
stands tremulous, shilly-shallying from the gutter, impet-
uous Ruskin plunges his rapier up to the very hilt in the

abominable belly of the vast blockheadism, and leaves it staring very considerably.'

Ruskin's address was in the spirit of his letter to the *Daily Telegraph*—less a defence of Eyre than an attack upon Radical callousness to the plight of the British workingman and overall Radical hypocrisy. His purpose in joining the Committee, Ruskin told the members assembled, was to obtain justice for men of every race. He detested all cruelty and deemed it cruel to drag blacks from their homes to labour in the fields, but more cruel to turn a white family off their home so that a shorter road might be built over their hearth. He could not, in all good conscience, join in a cry of condemnation of Eyre raised by the 'wholesale' murderers of white Englishmen. Mill and his political economist associates had insisted that to hang Gordon on suspicion was the same as murder. They would soon see if this were the case. During that past year, a drunken workman had staggered late one night, through the gate of the town house of a London gentleman. That gentleman, seeing the drunk in his garden, had shot him dead—on 'suspicion.' A jury had completely absolved him of any wrong-doing. This was the state of the law. And yet, what did John Stuart Mill say in his supremely logical fashion—and Ruskin proceeded to put these words in the mouth of his adversary:

> For the protection of your own person, and of a few feet of your own property, it is lawful for you to take life, on so much suspicion as may arise from a shadow cast on the wrong side of your wall. But for the safety, not of your own poor person, but of sixteen thousand men, women, and children, confiding in your protection, and entrusted to it; and for the guardianship not of your own stairs and plate-chest, but of a province involving in its safety that of all the English possessions in the West Indies—for these minor ends it is not lawful for you to take a single life on suspicion, though the suspicion rest, not on a shadow on the wall, but on experience of the character and conduct of the accused during many previous years.

(Ruskin's was a powerful argument, no doubt, yet its strength was not appreciated by the peers and colonels who had assembled to listen to it. What they had come to hear and were fully prepared to cheer, was a thunderous declaration of loyalty to the Queen and a ringing denunciation of cowardly 'niggers.')

If Eyre had lost Jamaica, Ruskin continued, then he might with some justice have been removed from office. But to have been superseded after having saved Jamaica—this 'was an act of national imbecility which has not hitherto had its parallel in history.' The removal of Eyre, he asserted, was the act—as the threat of prosecution was the cry—of

a nation blinded by avarice to all true valour and virtue, and haunted, therefore, by phantoms of both; it was the suicidal act of a people, which, for the sake of filling its pockets, would pour mortal venom into all its air and all its streams; would shorten the lives of its labourers by thirty years a life, that it might get needle-packets two pence each cheaper; would communicate its liberty to foreign nations by forcing them to buy poison at the cannon's mouth, and prove its chivalry to them by shrinking in panic from the side of a people being slaughtered.

Frightened by their consciences, overwhelmed by the burden of such great guilt, the Radicals hoped to atone for their sins by rewarding 'with ruin the man who had dared to strike down one seditious leader, and rescue the lives of a population.' The believers in *laissez-faire* were determined to slaughter the scapegoat, Eyre, as a sacrifice before the immortal gods for the murders they committed in the ordinary course of a day's business.

There is no doubt that both Ruskin and Carlyle were sincere in the work they had undertaken. They had a high regard for Eyre himself. When the Governor was brought to meet him, Carlyle, after a careful inspection found him truly of the stuff of which heroes were made, and pronounced him 'a brave, gentle, chivalrous, and clear man, whom I would make dictator of Jamaica for the next twenty-five years were I now king of it.' Yet, Carlyle felt, Eyre had 'something of Grandison in him, mildly perceptible,' and that that was 'his limiting condition.' Ruskin was no less taken with Eyre. 'From all I have heard of Mr Eyre's career,' he wrote, 'I believe that his humanity and kindness of heart, his love of justice and mercy, and his eminently Christian principles, qualified him in a very high degree for the discharge of his arduous and painful duties at a most critical period of the history of the colony whose government he had to administer.' When, in late September, George Price, whom we have already encountered as Eyre's antagonist in the Tramway affair of 1862, wrote to Ruskin and set forth the details of this unsavoury episode, Ruskin had been shaken by this information from a source he deemed reliable. Carlyle was given Price's letters and, after studying them, decided that the Tramway Scandal was thoroughly inconsequential, that it was 'a *misbirth* of that nearly inconceivable little *Chaos in a Coalbox*,' the Jamaica House of Assembly. Relieved at Carlyle's judgment, Ruskin, though certainly *wanting* to believe it correct, nevertheless had qualms, which, strangely, were put to rest when Alexander Hume read to him a letter from Eyre which included a none too flattering estimate of Price.

But similarly unpleasant facts came to light which troubled Ruskin, who once confessed, in a letter to Carlyle, how badly some of his confidence in the Eyre cause had been undermined. It became more and more difficult for him to work as diligently as he had at the beginning, but he continued to fulfill the obligation he had undertaken rather than back out and disappoint either the Governor or Carlyle. An entry in Ruskin's diary during this period reads 'Doing my duty as well as I can for Governor Eyre.' But it was hard to do one's duty, when confidence has been shaken and when no one else seemed willing to share the burden. Ruskin became particularly annoyed at Charles Kingsley's silent licking of wounds incurred at Southampton. In a letter written twenty years later, Ruskin revealed his disgust: Kingsley, he was to write, had 'failed in the most cowardly way when we had the Eyre battle to fight' and had shown himself to be a 'flawed—partly rotten, partly distorted—person.' On still another occasion, when Kingsley's conduct after Southampton was being discussed in company, Ruskin remarked that 'I never thought much of muscular Christianity after that.'

Soon, too soon, Ruskin had cause to feel dissatisfied with Carlyle as well. Although the old man was quite willing to lend his name to the Committee, and to give it mountains of advice, he would not assume any share of the work. All this, he left to Ruskin and—in spite of the latter's devotion to his master—the younger man felt put upon. Most especially was this so during the early months of 1867 when Carlyle left upon a trip to the continent. William Rossetti, the artist-friend of John Ruskin, noted, in early 1867, that 'Carlyle got Ruskin to join the Eyre Defence Fund by urging him to second Carlyle in that body, and that Ruskin now considers himself somewhat left in the lurch by Carlyle's absence in Italy, while Ruskin, who would willingly have kept out of the whole affair, remains here to bear the brunt.'

On top of all these difficulties was a growing dissatisfaction with the services of the Committee's Secretary, Hamilton Hume. At one point, both Ruskin and Carlyle were interested in having Hume's services 'supplemented' by the employment of another and more capable person, but Hume was so disturbed and disconcerted at the suggestion of such 'help,' that the proposal was allowed to die. But despite all—despite Ruskin's loss of confidence, the 'cowardice' of Kingsley, the irresponsibility of Carlyle, and Hume's inefficiency—the efforts of the Eyre Defence Committee were fairly successful. A very considerable amount of money was received in every mail by Committee headquarters. More important, perhaps, in the light of the character that the controversy had assumed, was the success that the Eyre Committee enjoyed in its name-hunting. Among the persons who, in the first months following the organization of the Committee, agreed to lend their names as well as their funds to the Eyre cause was the most popular poet of the day, the Poet Laureate, Ten-

nyson, and England's most popular novelist, Charles
Dickens.

Alfred Tennyson sent his subscription to the Eyre Defence Fund in October 1866 as 'a tribute to the nobleness
of the man, and as a protest against the spirit in which a
servant of the State, who has saved for us one of the Islands of the Empire, and many English lives, seems to be
hunted down.' The Eyre Committee had approached Tennyson and asked for his help and he had decided to give
it only after long and hard thought. The question in the
poet's mind was whether revolution and massacre could
have been prevented by a less harsh policy. He had come
to the conclusion that it would not have been possible to
do so. Tennyson did add one qualification to his support,
however: 'my entering my name on your Committee
might be looked upon as a pledge that I approve of all
the measures of Governor Eyre. I cannot assert that I do
this, neither would I say that he has erred, my knowledge
of the circumstances not being sufficient.' 'The outbreak of
our Indian Mutiny,' Tennyson wrote in conclusion, 'remains as a warning to all but mad men against want of
vigour and swift decisiveness.' In the battle between hu-
manitarianism and the needs of the empire which had
been waged in the heart of the Poet Laureate, the empire
had won out.

As for Charles Dickens, a recent biographer has attributed his support of Eyre to the influence of Thomas
Carlyle, an influence which for many years was paramount
in determining the novelist's political views. Dickens regarded the Jamaica insurrection as another example of
government ignorance and neglect of most grievous conditions and thought of his contribution to the Defence
Fund as a protest against this ignorance. There were cor-
roborating factors. Dickens had been a long-time opponent
of Radicalism, sharing the view of both Ruskin and Carlyle
that *laissez-faire* had been guilty of murdering and maim-
ing countless workingmen. He had depicted and carica-
tured the heartless social outlook of Radicalism in the
character of Scrooge, in *A Christmas Carol*, contrasting it
with Old England's warm and bountiful spirit of Christmas

past. In *Bleak House*, he had pictured Mrs Jellyby, a lady who, in her anxiety to do good works to promote the Brotherhood of Humanity and the condition of the natives of Africa, had badly neglected her own home—an indictment of the devotees of Exeter Hall. (In an article, written in 1848, Dickens had asserted that 'it might be laid down as a very good general rule of social and political guidance that whatever Exeter Hall champions, is the thing by no means to be done.') In *Barnaby Rudge* and *A Tale of Two Cities*, he had portrayed the mad, terrifying behaviour of a mob in terms not very different from Carlyle's. Was it surprising that Dickens joined his old friend Carlyle in backing Eyre against chaos, the Radicals, and Exeter Hall? Dickens, however, simply lent his name, and did not take an active part in the work of the Eyre Committee.

The Liberal press was horrified at the support given to Eyre by England's most prominent men of letters. 'It is of little importance that men of the stamp of Lord Cardigan should patronize wholesale illegality,' one journalist expostulated. 'Nothing better is expected of them. But Mr Carlyle, and even Mr Ruskin, occupy a far other place in the public estimation, and exercise a far other influence than [Cardigan] . . . to whose level for the moment they have descended.' The Liberal *Economist* detailed its grievances against the Sage of Chelsea:

> Mr Carlyle's defence of Mr Eyre means, if it means anything, that we are to reverse our system of government by law, based as nearly as may be on principles of justice, sweep away all safeguards of personal liberty, and set up instead the will of one man, who may be an Aristides, but who may also be an Eyre. . . .

If Carlyle's and Ruskin's sponsorship of Eyre resulted in a general acceptance of the ex-Governor's conduct, 'then the less these very highly cultivated persons intervene the better for us and them, for they would stand quite as good a chance of sharing the fate of Gordon as we or any other of Her Majesty's subjects.' 'It is absolutely necessary,' it said in conclusion, 'in the interest of the highest as well as the meanest of Englishmen that the contemptuous disregard of the safeguards of personal liberty shown by Mr Carlyle and his colleagues should receive public reprobation. . . .'

During the last few months of 1866, friends of the Jamaica Committee had let it be known that the Eyre group had already collected £10,000. The rumour grew and it was reported as fact by *The Times*. The day following this report, Sir Roderick Murchison, the gentleman-geologist who served as one of the vice-presidents of the Eyre Fund, hastened to write—lest potential contributors feel that no more money was needed—that his Committee had only collected £4,000 as yet and that much more would be required. With counter-malice, the Eyre Defence and Aid Fund wrote potential subscribers that the Jamaica Committee had raised £10,000 and that friends of Governor Eyre had better hustle to match this sum. Newspaper advertisements were used to reach potential subscribers, and the Eyre Fund printed the names of large subscribers, and of prominent persons who donated to its fund regardless of the size of subscriptions. Circulars were sent to 'all those who believe that Governor Eyre quelled the insurrection in Jamaica, and saved that island, to come forward and boldly proclaim such to be their opinion.' The executive of the Eyre Fund wrote to every officer who commanded a regiment of Volunteers to ask for help in collecting subscriptions, informing them that the attack upon Eyre was an attack upon constitutional law and order which made them and all other 'respectable' persons its target.

When, after the conclusion of the Jamaica prosecutions, the Eyre Defence Fund announced the names of those who had made contributions to its treasury, the list was found to include seventy-one peers, six bishops, twenty M.P.'s, forty generals, twenty-six admirals, four hundred clergymen (principally, Church of England), and 30,000 other individuals. Many of the Eyre Committee's most celebrated contributors took no active part in its work, and even Carlyle, as we have seen, was content to watch from afar. Soon, Ruskin, too, burdened and a trifle discouraged, left the Committee's work to other, more willing, hands;

though Carlyle, not infrequently, sauntered forth to dictate
a course of action, his suggestions often seemed so unwise,
they were ignored. The everyday work of the Eyre Committee fell upon men like Murchison.

Sir Roderick Murchison was a septuagenarian and the
dean, the grand old man of British science. Not an academic scholar like Huxley or Tyndall, but a gentleman-
savant, a geologist who had achieved recognition and
even distinction in his field. At this time, he was, and had
been for some years, the President of the Geographical
Society; in 1868, he was elected President of the British
Association. Murchison was a wealthy man, of considerable social influence, whose home on Belgrave Square was
a meeting place not only for men of science and letters,
but for cabinet ministers and distinguished peers. His
scientific acumen was much admired by the fox-hunting
gentlemen whose sport, in off-season months, was politics.
But throughout his life, Murchison remained very much
the country squire who happened to have a passion for
rocks rather than for antique firearms, and who spent his
time collecting the facts of geology rather than those of
genealogy. He had received a knighthood in 1846, a bar-
onetcy some years later, and a volley of honorary degrees.
Cabinet ministers could be sure he understood them, and
on the most crucial scientific issues of the day, he was
sure to be 'safe'. On evolution, for example, his views were
entirely opposed to those of Lyell and Darwin and in sub-
stantial agreement with those of Bishop Wilberforce, although he took care not to take prominent part in the
public debate on the subject.

By the end of 1867, the membership of the Jamaica Committee had grown from the previous year's total of 300
to over 800 gentlemen. In its literature, the Committee
referred to itself as 'The Ten Thousand Pounds Fund'—
that being the sum it hoped to raise for the Eyre prosecution. The year also saw an increase in the number of aca-
demicians who subscribed to the Committee's programme
and coffers: among them were Albert Venn Dicey, a Fellow of Trinity College, Cambridge; the blind Henry Faw-

cett, the professor of political economy at Cambridge and a Liberal M.P. to boot; Sir Edward Frankland, professor of chemistry at the Royal Institution; T. H. Green, the neo-Hegelian philosopher and a Fellow of Balliol College, Oxford; Thorold Rogers, a political economist from Oxford.

To raise money for the prosecution against Eyre, the Regius Professor of History at Oxford, Goldwin Smith undertook a lecture tour, principally in the North of England, in the early part of 1867. He delivered a series of four lectures, one on Pym, one on Cromwell, and two on the younger Pitt to large and friendly audiences. The first two lectures reminded Englishmen of that time when men had been willing to sacrifice lives and fortunes for the cause of liberty. In his Cromwell lecture, Smith said: 'Of the religion of hero-worship, I am no devotee. . . . Great men are most precious gifts of heaven, and unhappy is the nation which cannot produce them at its need. But their importance in history becomes less as civilization goes on.' He confessed himself happy to pay homage to the historian Carlyle who had written the *French Revolution*: 'that work is his best, partly because it is free from a hero.' Carlyle's subsequent book on Cromwell, however, was quite otherwise: it 'is hero-worship, and therefore it is not true.' 'Carlyle,' Smith concluded, 'prostrates morality before greatness. His imitators prostrate it before mere force, which is no more adorable than mere fraud, the force of those who are physically weak. We might as well bow down before the hundred-handed idol of a Hindoo. To moral force we may bow down: but moral force resides and can reside in those only whose lives embody the moral law. It is found in the highest degree in those at whom hero-worship sneers.'

So far as men of letters were concerned, the Eyre forces had an overpowering lead: Carlyle, Ruskin, Tennyson, Dickens, and Kingsley. The Jamaica Committee could only reply weakly with Tom Hughes, who had no real claim to literary eminence, and John Stuart Mill, less a 'literary' man than a philosopher and economist. But if the Eyre Committee had the better claim to literary distinction, it was the Jamaica Committee which attracted the chief men of science. The father of evolution, Charles Darwin, and his loyal disciple, the biologist, Thomas Henry Huxley, as well as the noted geologist, Charles Lyell, were all members of the Jamaica Committee. The Eyre Defence Committee could only boast of Carlyle's old friend, the physicist John Tyndall, who was a teacher and popularizer of the sciences, more a 'literary' man than a scientist, and the covert support of Joseph Hooker.

Perhaps it was natural for the scientists to enlist themselves in the middle-class Jamaica Committee. The middle-classes had welcomed scientific advance, 'progress'; the gentry and aristocracy had tended to distrust a 'progress' which was devouring special privileges. There was, moreover, a difference of views between the two camps on a vital scientific subject—evolution. During the 'sixties, the question of evolution was the most significant and most widely discussed scientific matter, and the discussion ranged far beyond scientific circles. The keenest public controversy developed about the question. The chief proponents of evolution—Darwin, Huxley, Lyell, and Herbert Spencer—were all to be found in the ranks of the Jamaica Committee, while many of its leading opponents, literary, ecclesiastical, and scientific, were adherents of Governor Eyre. In a roundabout way, it appeared natural that the evolutionists should ally themselves with the Radicals: they both owed much to the 'dismal science' of political economy. For mid-nineteenth century Radicalism, the precepts developed by Malthus and Ricardo were the final word in economic reasoning, and, as it happened, the key principle of the evolutionists—the survival of the fittest— had also been derived from the economics of Malthus. It was the operation of this principle in English economic life that Ruskin had deplored.

The publication of *The Origin of Species* in November 1859 had initiated a controversy which was to last for many years. There had been roars of opposition, especially from the Church. Darwin was a shy man, unwilling to take too prominent a part in the controversy. Thomas Henry Huxley, therefore, a young doctor and naturalist, became the chief protagonist of the evolutionists; he called himself 'Darwin's bulldog' and took upon himself the burden of yipping and barking at all attackers. The strongholds of 'conservatism,' in thought as well as in politics, were the established Church, the aristocracy, and the military, and these groups had the least sympathy with the evolutionists. Disraeli spoke for them when he described the controversy as a debate as to whether men had descended from apes or from angels, and proclaimed himself 'on the side of the angels.' Among literary men, Carlyle made no secret of his contempt for evolutionary doctrine. Although at one time he and Huxley had been friends, indeed Huxley, like so many talented young men of the day had regarded Carlyle as his mentor, Carlyle's profound distaste for evolution had put an end to their relationship. Many years after the end of the Eyre Case, Huxley was to see Carlyle hobbling down the opposite side of a London street. The old man looked lonely and Huxley crossed to greet him. Carlyle looked up sharply and acidly remarked 'You're Huxley, aren't you? The man that says we're all descended from monkeys.'

It is curious to note that those denounced in their own day as hard men of science, men who cultivated facts and eschewed sentiment, were all ranged on the 'sentimental' side of the Eyre controversy. On the other hand, the poets and writers, including the chief 'apostle of feeling,' Thomas Carlyle, were as uniformly ranged on the side which extolled brute strength as a heroic virtue. Furthermore, it was the evolutionists, the theorists of the struggle for existence and survival of the fittest, who protested against the operation of just these principles in Jamaica, while the opponents of evolutionary doctrine turned out to be advocates of a primitive 'social-Darwinism.' There were, indeed, to be two species of social-Darwinism. One might be called 'internal,' was to become identified with Herbert Spencer, vaunted economic competition; this was endorsed by the leading Radicals. The other, 'external,' concerned itself with wars between nations and races, and was implicit in Carlyle's view of the 'rights' acquired because of English superiority over the 'niggers' of Jamaica, and thirty years later became explicit in both Benjamin Kidd's and Karl Pearson's defences of British imperialism.

The founder of evolution, Charles Darwin, felt strongly about the Eyre Case. In November 1866, he became a member of the Jamaica Committee and subscribed to its funds. One of Darwin's sons recounts a conversation with the eminent biologist during the height of the agitation. The young man had decided that it was perhaps too strong a measure to prosecute Eyre for murder and, in the manner of young men, flippantly suggested that the Jamaica Committee spend the money it had already collected on a dinner. 'My father turned on me almost with fury,' the son recounted some years later. If he wanted a dinner, Darwin asserted, he had 'better go back to Southampton.' The unusual sharpness of Darwin's retort put an end to further conversation for that evening. At seven o'clock the following morning, Darwin knocked at his son's bedroom door. The founder of evolution had been unable to sleep the entire night because he had spoken so harshly and had come to apologize.

Huxley, 'Darwin's bulldog,' was delighted that his 'master' had come out, as he later wrote Darwin, 'on the right (that is *my*) side in the Jamaica business.' He was particularly pleased because the Jamaica affair had already separated so many friends; 'it is wonderful,' he wrote, 'how people who commonly act together are divided about it.' Huxley was forty at the time of the Jamaica insurrection, and one of England's leading naturalists. When *The Origin of Species* had been published, he had been quick to recognize that it gave a valid and sufficient explanation for the development of forms of life and rapidly became the outstanding British advocate of evolutionary doctrine. His reputation grew, and in 1863, he had become Hunterian Professor at the Royal College of Surgeons as well as Fullerian Professor at the Royal Institution. When the noted man of science announced his position on the question of Governor Eyre in the autumn of 1866, his views—some of which were a bit disconcerting—were received with considerable interest. The *Pall Mall Gazette* of 29th October 1886, made an allusion to the part taken in the

affair by Huxley which brought a quick reply from the
biologist. The *Gazette* had reported that Sir Charles Lyell
and Huxley had given their support to the Jamaica Committee, and added that 'It would be curious also to know
how far Sir Charles Lyell's and Mr Huxley's peculiar views
on the development of species have influenced them in
bestowing on the negro that sympathetic recognition
which they are willing to extend even to the ape as "a
man and a brother."' Huxley replied, on October 31st:

I have been induced to join . . . [the Jamaica Com-
mittee] neither by my 'peculiar views on the development of species,' nor by any particular love for, or
admiration of the negro—still less by any miserable desire to wreak vengeance for recent error upon a man
whose early career I have often admired. . . .

I do not presume to speak with authority on a legal
question; but, unless I am misinformed, English law
does not permit good persons, as such, to strangle bad
persons, as such. On the contrary, I understand that,
if the most virtuous of Britons, let his place and authority be what they may, seize and hang up the greatest
scoundrel in Her Majesty's dominions simply because
he is an evil and troublesome person, an English court
of justice will certainly find that virtuous person guilty
of murder.

. . . . I entertain so deeply-rooted an objection to
this method of killing people—the act itself appears to
me to be so frightful a precedent, that I desire to see it
stigmatized by the highest authority as a crime. And I
have joined the committee which proposed to indict
Mr Eyre, in the hope that I may hear a court of justice
declare that the only defence which can be set up (if
the Royal Commissioners are right) is no defence, and
that the killing of Mr Gordon was the greatest offence
known to the law—murder.

In a letter to his friend Charles Kingsley, who, of course,
opposed him on this issue, Huxley explained his stand
more fully:

Jermyn Street, Nov. 8, 1866.

MY DEAR KINGSLEY—

. . . . I desire to see Mr Eyre indicted and
a verdict of guilty in a criminal court obtained . . .
because a new study of all the evidence which has now
been collected has confirmed my first conviction that
Gordon's execution was as bad a specimen as we have
had since Jeffreys' time of political murder. . . .

He [Eyre] is as much responsible for Gordon's death
as if he had shot him through the head with his own
hand. I daresay he did all this with the best of motives,
and in a heroic vein. But if English law will not declare
that heroes have no more right to kill people in this
fashion than other folk, I shall take an early opportunity
of migrating to Texas or some other quiet place where
there is less hero-worship and more respect for
justice. . . .

In point of fact, men take sides on this question, not so
much by looking at the mere facts of the case, but
rather as their deepest political convictions lead them.
And the great use of the prosecution, and one of my
reasons for joining it, is that it will help a great many
people to find out what their profoundest political
beliefs are.

The hero-worshippers who believe that the world is to
be governed by its great men, who are to lead the little
ones, justly if they can; but if not, unjustly drive or kick
them the right way, will sympathise with Mr Eyre.

The other sect (to which I belong) who look upon hero-
worship as no better than any other idolatry, and upon
the attitude of mind of the hero-worshipper as essen-
tially immoral; who think it is better for a man to go
wrong in freedom than to go right in chains; who look
upon the observance of inflexible justice as between
man and man as of far greater importance than even
the preservation of social order, will believe that Mr
Eyre has committed one of the greatest crimes of which
a person in authority can be guilty, and will strain every

nerve to obtain a declaration that their belief is in accordance with the law of England. . . . (author's italics)

Ever yours faithfully,
T. H. HUXLEY

Huxley's friend, Tyndall, had a very different view of the Eyre case. John Tyndall stemmed from a poor, Protestant family in Ireland. When in his early twenties, he had read *Past and Present* and had become a fervent admirer of Carlyle, later attributing his decision to follow a scientific career to the older man's influence. In 1853, Tyndall was appointed professor of natural philosophy, i.e., physics, in the Royal Institution and became a colleague of the great Faraday. He met another young scientist, Thomas Huxley, and the two became the closest of friends. In the ensuing years, Tyndall's reputation passed beyond academic walls. In widely attended public lectures, he was well able to describe, with charm and with lucidity, the phenomena of physics, and became a popular writer for laymen on scientific subjects.

It was in reply to an invitation to join the Jamaica Committee that Tyndall set out his views on the Eyre case. He had considered the facts most carefully, he reported, and had discovered that he agreed with his mentor Carlyle as to the laziness and viciousness of the Jamaica negroes, the dangers arising from the conspiracy, and Gordon's culpability. He asked the Jamaica Committee to note Eyre's circumstances in October 1865:

. . . . I am not prepared to deny that the period of punishment was too long, or that its character was too severe. Now that the smoke of battle has cleared away, you perhaps see more truly the character of the field. But I would invite you to transport yourselves to that field while the smoke still hung upon it . . . to think of Governor Eyre with the blood of his slaughtered countrymen before his eyes . . . with the consciousness that the whole island round him was near its point of combustion, and with no possible means of estimating how *near.* In what way, gentlemen, some of your number would have acted under these circumstances, God only knows. In all probability they would have acted kindly and calamitously, for philanthropists can unconsciously become shedders of blood. [Eyre was] obliged to augment his relative strength, by damping everywhere the spirit of rebellion, and this could only be done by making the name, power, and determination of England terrible throughout the island.

. . . . And such being my notions, when asked to join the Eyre Defence Committee, I felt that cowardice, or a dislike to the worry involved in the act, was the only reason which opposed my doing so. Concluding from what I had observed in society, that Governor Eyre was more likely to suffer from timidity than from conviction—that the dread of you, gentlemen, and of those whom you represent, was very widely spread—I overcame my strong reluctance to mingle in any matter of the kind. . . . I call upon you in the name of all that is wise and dignified in human nature—in the name of all that is just and manly in the English character— not to permit the folly of Governor Eyre's admirers, if such folly should, in your estimation exist, to colour your judgment in this grave question. And whether you will hear, or whether you will forbear, I call upon the men of England who share the views here set forth, to throw themselves without delay between you and Governor Eyre, and to prevent you from adding to the harm which he has already experienced at your hands.

After the 'retirement' of Ruskin and Carlyle, the Eyre Committee was forced to rely heavily upon John Tyndall and, indeed, in 1867, he was the intellectual 'lion' of the Eyre forces. Peers and generals were rarely articulate, and, being men of some dignity, were conscious of their penchant for placing their feet—whether buskined in ermine or shod in military boots—in their mouths. They were relieved that Tyndall would provide 'meat' for their meetings. In one Eyre Committee session, Tyndall announced support for the Governor's cause from a new and surprising source. Tyndall quoted from a personal letter of Dr Joseph Dalton Hooker, a botanist friend and aide of Darwin, who had decided to join the defence of Eyre. Hooker had set down in this letter what his friendship with both Darwin and Huxley had up to that time prevented him from stating in public: 'the negro in Jamaica [Hooker had written] . . . is pestilential, I have no hesitation in declaring; . . . he is a dangerous savage at the best.' In a second letter, Hooker had pronounced 'the liberty given to him [the negro] on Jamaica . . . detrimental to the prosperity of that island.' 'With testimony of which this is but a sample before me,' Tyndall argued, 'I decline accepting the negro as the equal of the Englishman, nor will I commit myself to the position that a negro and an English insurrection ought to be treated in the same way. . . .'

Tyndall continued: 'We do not hold an Englishman and a Jamaica negro to be convertible terms, nor do we think that the cause of human liberty will be promoted by any attempt to make them so.'

It is constantly urged by the supporters of the Jamaica Committee that the execution of Gordon is a frightful precedent. . . . Now I would beg to say that if the precedent be restricted to Jamaica, and to men of Gordon's stamp, who provoke insurrection there about four times in a century, it is not frightful, and if it be extended to England the extension is unwarrantable. Who dreams of making Jamaica a precedent for England? Certainly not the defenders of Mr Eyre.

Tyndall's statement was not true of Carlyle who had no objection to making the handling of the Jamaica mob a precedent for the handling of its English counterpart.

Tyndall was much concerned about how his stand in this matter might affect his friendship with Huxley. When he had written his letter to the Jamaica Committee, he had also penned a note to Huxley further explaining his position and expressing the wish and the hope that their friendship would not be damaged. For his part, Huxley was also anxious to keep the friendship whole, and answered Tyndall's note immediately.

MY DEAR TYNDALL,

Many thanks for the kind note which accompanied your letter to the Jamaica Committee.

When I presented myself at Rogers' dinner last night I had not heard of the latter, and Gassiot began poking fun at me, and declaring that your absence was due to a quarrel between us on this unhappy subject.

I replied to the jest earnestly enough, that I hoped and believed our old friendship was strong enough, to stand any strain that might be put on it, much as I grieved that we should be ranged in opposite camps in this or any other cause.

That you and I have fundamentally different political principles must, I think, have become obvious to both of us during the progress of the American War. The fact is made still more plain by your printed letter, the tone and spirit of which I greatly admired without being able to recognize in it any important fact or argument which had not passed through my mind before I joined the Jamaica Committee.

Thus there is nothing for it but for us to agree to differ, each supporting his own side to the best of his ability, and respecting his friend's freedom as he would his own, and doing his best to remove all petty bitterness from that which is at bottom one of the most important constitutional battles in which Englishmen have for many years been engaged.

If you and I are strong enough and wise enough, we shall be able to do this, and yet preserve that love for one another which I value as one of the good things of my life.

If not, we shall come to grief. I mean to do my best.

Ever yours faithfully,

T. H. HUXLEY

6

THE CONSTITUTION,
THE 'RABBLE'
AND THE EMPIRE

In his letter to Tyndall, Huxley had referred to the case of Governor Eyre as 'at bottom one of the most important constitutional battles in which Englishmen have for many years been engaged.' John Stuart Mill joined in that view: 'The question was,' he wrote, 'whether the British dependencies, and eventually, perhaps, Great Britain itself, were to be under the government of law, or of military license.' Both Mill and Hughes in Parliament—and other Jamaica Committee stalwarts, in the press, at public meetings, and in lecture halls—were to emphasize this constitutional issue. Yet to no avail, for the British public refused to believe its liberties threatened by the 'illegalities' of Governor Eyre. The philosopher Herbert Spencer, another active member of the Jamaica Committee, was exasperated, and completely failed to comprehend, as he wrote in his autobiography many years afterwards, how 'cultivated Englishmen should not have perceived that the real question at issue was whether free institutions were to be at the mercy of a chief magistrate'; this 'seems at first marvellous,' but, he added, 'it is marvellous only on the supposition that men's judgments are determined by reason, when they are in far larger measure determined by feelings.'

The question most directly at issue was martial law. The backers of the Jamaica Committee maintained that martial law had no place within the English legal system, while the supporters of Governor Eyre assigned to it a semi-mystical position, a code above and anterior to all other law. Frederic Harrison, a barrister, a defender of the legal rights of the trade unions, and one of the principal leaders of British positivism, was the Jamaica Committee's spokesman on this issue. There were other positivists among the members of the Jamaica Committee. There were Henry Crompton and Godfrey Lushington, both barristers, and Edward Spencer Beesly, the Professor of History at University College, London. Positivism, the so-called 'religion of humanity' set forth by August Comte a score of years earlier, was a matter of contention for mid-Victorian intellectuals. In 1866, Mill, after having first flirted with it, had denounced Comte's system as undemocratic, based as it was upon the rule of a High-Priest of Humanity and a patriciate of industrialists; Huxley described it as 'Catholicism minus Christianity,' since Comte had modelled much of the ritual and organizational structure of the religion of positivism upon Catholicism. Yet positivism laboured to foster a sense of social responsibility in the ruling class and bade industrialists watch over the welfare of the workers. English positivists supported the cause of trade-unionism in order to demonstrate the advantages of conciliation and of social peace. So far as immediate, practical programme was concerned, the positivists found themselves in agreement with the Radicals: advocates of free speech, so that they could preach their cause, supporters of the disestablishment of the Church of England, proponents of free, public secular education, anti-aristocratic, humanitarians, and, as members of an international church, cosmopolitan and anti-imperialistic, it was natural that they should find themselves drawn to the wing of Liberalism which shared these views. Although in theory, they may have subscribed to Comte's benevolent despotism of the capitalist patriciate, in practice the English positivists became advocates of votes for workingmen—believing suffrage reform necessary to counteract socially irresponsible aristocratic governments. The positivists' fight against Eyre was motivated by a desire to foster a spirit of social responsibility and to stimulate those feelings of humanity which, they felt, were necessary to prepare for the new Comtian utopia.

In November and December 1866, Frederic Harrison wrote a series of six letters to the *Daily News*, on his own initiative, as he took care to make clear, having consulted neither his fellow members of the Executive Committee nor its legal counsel. He described an early eighteenth-century case involving a carpenter attached to an army unit at Gibraltar who had been tried and sentenced by court martial for a military offence. It had been a fair trial and the commander of Gibraltar at the time, a Governor Sabine, had confirmed the sentence. The carpenter returned to England and brought an action against Sabine for illegal punishment of a civilian by court martial, and the Governor had been compelled to pay the carpenter £700 damages. Gordon had not been attached to the army, had been arrested in a district where martial law was not in operation, had for a long time been involved in a political struggle with Governor Eyre, and, moreover, his trial had been patently unfair. Indeed, there had been 439 similar courts martial in Jamaica. Yet, Harrison expostulated, the peers and the hierarchy of the Established Church had hailed Governor Eyre as a hero. What made the whole business 'critical' was that 'the bulk of English society positively desired to lodge in the hands of the Executive latent and indefinite prerogatives, which it was the boast of our forefathers to have destroyed.' Society did not mean to turn these abusive powers upon itself, upon Englishmen. What was 'insidious' was that these prerogatives 'are meant to maintain our vast unresting empire.'

In his letters, Harrison cited precedent after precedent to prove his propositions that the Crown had no power to suspend the civil law in Great Britain, and that martial law was unknown to the British legal system, and, in fact, had been condemned both by the common and by the statute law. A rebel could be legally killed in the fighting which accompanied the suppression of a rebellion, but if captured, had to be tried by civil not martial law. If a civilian were hung under martial law, it was plainly a case of murder. Furthermore, all officials, whether civil or

military, were responsible for every breach of the law and
could be held to account for their conduct. Harrison cited
precedents to prove that martial law did not exempt its
enforcers from prosecution—even after an act of indemnity
had been passed—if their conduct had exhibited deviation
from the common principles of humanity. There was no
doubt, he insisted, that Eyre's activities constituted a gross
breach of the law. So far as Gordon was concerned, 'English history, from Magna Charta to this day, can show no
case of accumulated violation of law by rulers so enormous
as this—short of acts of real assassination.'

'English law is of that kind, that, if you play fast and
loose with it, it vanishes. . . . What is done in a colony
today may be done in Ireland tomorrow, and in England
hereafter. . . . The sacred principles for which the English people once fought and struggled we now invoke for
the loftier end of checking the English people themselves
from imitating the tyranny they crushed.' Harrison protested against what a contemporary journalist had called
the 'nigger' principle. Many Englishmen were indignant
that the Jamaica blacks should claim, or that any set of
Englishmen should claim for them, the rights of white
Englishmen. The stories of the atrocities committed by the
Indian mutineers of 1857 and by the Jamaican rebels had
convinced much of the public that only by weighty force,
crushingly exercised, would it be possible to maintain control over the semi-educated, barbarous, coloured races of
the Empire. It was felt that if the Empire were to prosper,
Englishmen must have the grit to make use of harsh
measures in the overseas colonies, measures which would
have been intolerable if employed in England. There was
a growing feeling among the middle classes that the
Empire was a valuable possession and that therefore it
would be injudicious to tie the hands of governors in dealing with rebellious coloured colonials. Clemency might encourage further attacks; too great severity was a fault, to
be sure, but a fault in the right direction.

But Harrison—and the Jamaica Committee—appealed to
the British conscience: 'The precise issue [Harrison wrote]
we raise is this—that through our empire the British rule

shall be the rule of law; that every British citizen, white, brown, or black in skin, shall be subject to definite, and not to indefinite powers.' The system which Britain was putting into operation in her colonies was a system of terrorism: persons were punished not because they were proved to have committed a crime but in order to discourage others. It was as much an organized reign of terror as that which the Jacobins had instituted. 'Come what may, our colonial rule shall not be bolstered up by useful excess or irresponsible force,' he wrote. What had corrupted the British Army since Waterloo had been its continual wars with half-civilized savages; its tone and temper had been degraded into a delight in slaughter. 'The terrible Indian rebellion has sown evil seeds enough in the military as well as in the civil system. It called out all the tiger in our race.' 'That wild beast,' Harrison concluded, 'must be caged again.'

For many Englishmen, the wild beast that required caging was the working-class rabble. Writing in the early part of 1867, Matthew Arnold declared 'I am very much struck with the alarmed conservative feeling I see growing up among the middle-class tradesmen and employers of labour. . . . Their disgust at Bright and the working class is as deep as that of the aristocratic world.' By the last months of 1866, it was clear that the enemies of Eyre were but a small minority of the educated and articulate classes of Great Britain, supported by the leaders of a part of the organized working classes. But the bulk of the middle classes, in seeming defiance of long-standing traditional constitutional principles, was virtually unanimous in its support of Eyre. The seventeenth-century struggle for liberty had been waged against the Stuart Kings. But in 1866, the 'royal' prerogative was exercised by cabinets which, if still controlled by the aristocracy, wielded power in the overall interest of the propertied classes, as a whole. Here was a tremendous change. Why should the upper and middle classes act to limit their own power? The mid-Victorian supporters of authority and aristocratic government were convinced that they *were* defending the

British constitution—defending it against the threat of revolution by the 'democratic rabble'—and during the years 1866 and 1867 there were ample grounds for their fears.

The riots at Hyde Park had their sequel in a series of demonstrations—peaceful but nevertheless menacing. The leaders of the suffrage fight—John Bright, Edmond Beales, John Stuart Mill, and Thomas Hughes—had determined to continue the dangerous strategy which they had commenced the preceding summer, convinced that the only way to persuade the Conservative Government to pass a Reform Bill was to demonstrate the determination of the great masses of workingmen. In the latter part of 1866, John Bright and Edmond Beales organized giant demonstrations in every part of the island, which only served to increase the fears and resentments of the middle-classes. As if the Reform agitation were not enough, with the coming of the new year of 1867, street agitation of a different sort began. On the evening of 24th January 1867, bread riots broke out at Greenwich and Deptford, eastern suburbs of London. The suspension in shipbuilding during the previous year had caused a great increase in unemployment, the winter of 1866-67 was a cold one, and the relief facilities were insufficient. On this winter's eve in late January, mobs of men went from street to street breaking into bakers' shops to get bread. A body of mounted police finally restored order. There were few things more odious to respectability than a mob loose—whether agitating for a vote or a loaf. And 1866 and 1867 had seen an unusually large number of mob demonstrations.

Fear of the rabble and of universal suffrage, and interest in maintaining, by terror if necessary, the riches of the empire, were ranged against the Radical defence of liberty and representative democracy. (In addition, there was Ruskin's rather personal position, charging the opponents of Governor Eyre with hypocrisy.) The Eyre case, of course, posed an important imperial question, and opinions on the matter were closely related to what was happening in the most troublesome part of the Empire—Ireland. If an anachronistic pun were permissible, it might be said that for much of English public opinion what was at issue in the controversy was not Eyre but Eire. In 1867 and 1868, the British newspapers were filled with stories of Fenian disturbances. After the parliamentary extension of the suffrage, Fenian raids replaced Reform riots as a chief source of worry. The possibility of insurrection in Ireland was real—and frightening. Governor Eyre had crushed a Jamaica insurrection and had kept that island within the Empire. If Eyre were convicted, would that not place an obstacle in the path of those entrusted with the task of keeping the peace in Ireland—and keeping an Ireland, more and more bent on Home Rule, within the United Kingdom?

After three Fenians were executed for killing a police sergeant in Manchester, in November 1867, impressive funeral demonstrations took place in cities throughout Ireland. In Dublin, British troops were confined to barracks to prevent trouble between them and the demonstrators. In December, an attempt by the Fenians to rescue two imprisoned comrades by blowing up the outer walls of the Clerkenwell House of Detention at London failed, but not without killing several innocent persons. A contemporary English observer remarked that 'the utter recklessness of human life which this outrage exhibited, and the determination it evinced on the part of the conspirators to disregard all scruples and sacrifices, in order to carry out the objects of their lawless undertaking, brought home to all loyal and well-disposed minds a conviction of the necessity of strengthening, by every legitimate means, the hands of the authorities, and asserting in the most emphatic manner the supremacy of the law.' The government appealed to all persons to enroll as special constables to help safeguard London against similar occurrences. Thousands of citizens were sworn in during the weeks following the Clerkenwell explosion.

During the early part of 1868, Michael Barrett, the man believed to have set off the Clerkenwell explosion, was tried at the Central Criminal Court. The prosecuting barrister was the brilliant and eloquent Hardinge Giffard. Barrett was found guilty and was hanged on the 26th of

May, at the last public execution in Great Britain. Other demonstrations of Fenian violence, even an attempt to assassinate the Duke of Edinburgh, one of Victoria's sons who was, at the time, touring Australia, greatly disturbed the English public.

The mood of that public can be gauged by a letter which the poet-critic, Matthew Arnold, wrote to his mother on 14th December 1867. Arnold's sympathies were clear:

> You know I have never wavered in saying that the Hyde Park business eighteen months ago was fatal, and that a Government which dared not deal with a mob, of any nation or with any design, simply opened the floodgates to anarchy. You cannot have one measure for Fenian rioting and another for English rioting, merely because the design of the Fenian rioting is more subversive and desperate; what the State has to do is to put down *all* rioting with a strong hand, or it is sure to drift into troubles.

The English governing classes in the 1860's regarded the Irish and the non-European 'native' peoples just as they had, quite openly, regarded their own labouring classes for many centuries: as thoroughly undisciplined, with a tendency to revert to bestial behaviour, consequently requiring to be kept in order by force, and by occasional but severe flashes of violence; vicious and sly, incapable of telling the truth, naturally lazy and unwilling to work unless under compulsion. The eighteenth-century writers on economic subjects never tire of insisting upon the incorrigible character—immoral, profligate—of the lower orders, and the persistence of their attempts to avoid work—just as Carlyle regarded Quashee—though the men of the eighteenth century did not attribute differences in industry, honesty, and integrity to race. Rather, it was generally assumed that the lower classes had been brutalized by their condition over the centuries. But, however caused, the result was the same: brutes they were and brutal methods were sometimes required to maintain con-

trol or society would degenerate to the state of the *bellum
omnium contra omnes.*

In the early eighteen-thirties, a British Radical, dis-
cussing the rash of agricultural disturbances in the southern
counties at that time, especially rick-burning, described
the methods of terror which had formerly been employed
in England to deal with uprisings of serfs, and which, he
wrote, were still employed in the Southern United States,
'and in the dominions of our friendly ally, the Emperor
of Russia.' The method was this:

Send troops into the blazing districts; proclaim martial
law; shoot, cut down, and hang the peasants by wholesale, and without discrimination.

'In this way,' he continued, 'we should be sure to strike the
guilty; and we might satisfy out consciences afterwards
by proving, what would be really indisputable, that most
of the innocent had been incendiaries at heart, and that
we had spared them the guilt of becoming actual burners.'
But, he wrote, such methods would no longer be tolerated
'by reason of the humanity of the middle classes, which
has lately grown to such a pitch, that it would now be
difficult to get up a second Manchester Massacre,' like that
in 1819, and it would be much more difficult to get up
'an exterminating war upon the peasantry.' Furthermore,
'the very common soldiers have learned to think and feel
for others, so far, at least, as to be no longer blind
instruments of a strong, bad government,' and, moreover,
'public opinion . . . would not allow an evil disposed
government to use the old Anglo-Irish method of obtaining ease, by means of rebellion and massacre.'

If the humanity of the middle classes and the soldiery,
and of public opinion generally, had made unlikely the
use of such barbaric methods of dealing with active
domestic discontent, need a British government hesitate in
applying them to quell disturbances in Ireland, or in India,
or in the West Indies? Did humanitarian sentiment extend
over the seas? Did it extend to men of foreign tongues
and coloured skins? These were some of the questions to

which the case of Governor Eyre gave rise. Indeed, we must remember that even the English workman was still regarded as tied to a bare subsistence standard of living because of his penchant for drinking and tobacco, and John Stuart Mill—speaking before a meeting of workingmen in 1865—described that class as habitual liars. Nor had the growth of great industrial cities dampened the fears of Jacqueries. There had been rick-burning in the 'twenties and 'thirties, but even more dangerous than the diminishing numbers of agricultural labourers were the new congregations of urban workmen in the slums of the factory-towns of Lancashire and the Midlands. City mobs had terrified respectability in the rioting which had led to the passage of the Reform Bill of 1832 (which had enfranchised the bulk of the middle classes) and in the Chartist demonstrations of the later-'thirties and the 'forties which had vainly attempted to secure the vote for the working-man. The fear of class war, of the drawing up of barricades between the well-fed, educated minority and the ignorant, greedy masses, welled up in the agitation for the suffrage in the late 'sixties. In a deeper sense, there was an invisible barricade dividing what Disraeli described as 'the two nations,' the rich and the poor.

On 15th August 1867, the Reform Bill, having been finally passed by both Houses of Parliament, received the royal assent. The Radical strategy of bringing the workingmen out in force, by the hundreds of thousands, had made Reform an issue which neither party could safely neglect. The Radicals had posed the blunt threat of revolution and mass intimidation had worked. Many Tory leaders tended to go further in the direction of universal suffrage than had their Liberal counterparts: they had had enough of the breaking of Hyde Park railings and Trafalgar Square rallies—they wanted a solution of the suffrage question which would indeed be 'final.' After a complex process of committee reports and amendments, dramatically marked by resignations from the government and even the near-resignation of Gladstone from the Liberal leadership, the various restrictions which opponents of universal suffrage had placed in the bill had been weeded out. What had triumphed was 'household' suffrage, in effect universal manhood suffrage in the boroughs, a result which the majority of both parties had opposed at the beginning of the session. The city workingman had received the vote and the electorate was nearly doubled. One Conservative leader, Lord Cranborne, regarded the Reform Bill as the negation of all the principles of his party, and Disraeli called it, most frankly, 'a leap in the dark.' If the leap had not been made, Disraeli believed, if the Tory Government had not produced a Reform measure, the result would have been 'fatal not merely to the Conservative Party, but most dangerous to the country.' A Liberal enemy of Reform, Robert Lowe, prophesied doom. 'The bag which holds the winds,' said Lowe, 'will be untied, and we shall be surrounded by a perpetual whirl of change, alteration, innovation and revolution.' Reform did not extirpate deep, long-held suspicions of the 'rabble.' In some quarters, it intensified them.

For whatever reasons—whether because of the Reform agitation or because of Reform itself, or because of nameless, shapeless forces which had brought the suffrage issue to the centre of the political stage—Robert Lowe's prediction proved correct during 1867 and 1868. The coming of Reform did not halt mob violence, and the determination of the middle classes to oppose chaos hardened. These were turbulent years, for if the final passage of the Reform Bill had ended one source of trouble, there were others to take its place. Riot and murder were the order of the day. In Ireland and in England, the Fenians continued to make their raids; during 1867 and 1868, special constables were enlisted by the thousands to defend England against Fenian assaults. Religious riots were taking place in Birmingham, and there were frequent reports of trade union murders emanating from the industrial midlands. These last particularly shocked the middle classes.

In the younger, smaller trade unions of the Midlands, violent intimidation was frequently employed to 'persuade' unorganized workers to join the union or employers to agree to union conditions. A particularly lurid incident involved a Sheffield employer murdered by two hoodlums who had been hired by the Secretary of the Saw Grinder's Union, a man named Broadhead. The employer had refused to heed union complaints about his hiring too many young apprentices and Broadhead had decided to make an example of him. The middle and upper classes—the articulate, newspaper-reading classes of Great Britain—were shocked. There was talk of cracking down hard on the trade unions, even of driving the unions entirely from the industrial field. A Royal Commission appointed in 1867 to inquire into these conditions included Thomas Hughes, M.P., and Frederic Harrison. The larger, more responsible unions objected to being tarred with the same brush as the small, criminally-led unions of the Midlands, and relied upon Hughes and Harrison to persuade Parliament and the public to distinguish between the two kinds of unionism. The unions were much disturbed by a distinction which the public only too readily made, that between Broadhead, the trade union murderer of one employer, and Governor Eyre, whom the union leaders regarded as the murderer of hundreds of Jamaica blacks.

Professor Beesly, a friend of Harrison and a member of the Jamaica Committee, was much occupied with the problems of trade unionism, and, being an eloquent speaker, was frequently called upon to participate in labour meetings. On 2nd July 1867, Beesly was asked to speak at an Exeter Hall meeting called by the trade unions of London to protest against the illegalities of their Sheffield brethren. Speakers preceding Beesly had condemned the Sheffield system and the murderous Broadhead. Beesly, while denouncing Broadhead, took a less apologetic tack —much to the satisfaction of his workingman audience. 'Murder,' Beesly asserted, 'was a great crime, but they must not forget that the murder by trade unionists was no better and no worse than any other murder.' There were loud cheers from the audience. Beesly declared that he was no apologist for murder; in fact, during the past year, he had given money and worked hard 'to bring a great murderer to justice.' At this reference to the Eyre affair, there was still more cheering. 'This was a murderer,' the professor of history continued, 'whose hands were red with the blood of more than four hundred men, and this man committed his crimes in the interests of employers, as Broadhead committed his in the interest of the workmen of Sheffield.' There was prolonged cheering. Did the wealthy men of England 'meet as this meeting had met in Exeter Hall to say they abhorred these crimes?' No, they offered the murderer banquets. Governor Eyre now roamed free in England 'because magistrates of his own class refused to send his crimes to be tried by a jury.'

The workingmen in Exeter Hall shouted their approval of Beesly's words. The newspapers of the following day were vehement in their denunciations of the professor. Some journals appeared to believe that Beesly had not only defended the Sheffield murders but had actually incited his workingman audience to imitate Broadhead. Even the Radical papers objected to the positivist's appeal to 'class feeling.' Jamaica was immediately discounted by the pro-Eyre press as an anology to the Sheffield incident: there was no similarity between the cowardly Broadhead and the heroic Eyre. *Punch* urged the professor to change his name to *Beestly*. A move was immediately got underway to remove Beesly from his chair of history at University College, and although, in the weeks following, it gained considerable strength, it finally failed.

It was in such an atmosphere that the succession of events which became known to the public as the 'Jamaica prosecutions' proceeded. Under these conditions, the result of the prosecutions was hardly to be wondered at. By the middle of the nineteenth century, it did not do to publicly make 'provocative' statements about the manners and morals of the lower classes and the methods by which they had to be kept within bounds: by this time probably, most workingmen were literate, and were supplied by a multitude of newspapers and journals with the opinions of their betters. Free vent, however, could be given to such sentiments when their targets were the 'natives' of Great Britain's vast non-European colonial empire, and, indeed even the denizens of Ireland. The bulk of Englishmen were not offended by secular sermons upon the sly, vicious, lazy, lying Hindu or Celt, and how they had to be taught their place. If, by the eighteen-sixties, it had become dangerous to think of ruling the English working classes by the methods which were common as recently as the 'Peterloo Massacre' of 1819, it was still possible to speak openly, and to back words by deeds, of governing the 'niggers' of India or the West Indies or the Fenian Irish by the methods of terror by which the lower orders of Great Britain had been governed in previous centuries.

The case of Governor Eyre was perhaps the first in which it might be said that the realities of a heavy-handed imperial rule were confronted by the growing acceptance of democracy in the homeland.

There was a section of opinion on the Eyre case which deserves some discussion—and whose existence will satisfy some more cynical readers who may suspect the humanitarian and cosmopolitan sentiments of the antagonists of Governor Eyre. Although the leaders of Liberal opinion on the Eyre case were the decidedly anti-imperialist Cobdenites, there were other Liberals, following in the pattern set by the Radical economists of the first half of the century, of men like Robert Torrens, and Edward Gibbon Wakefield, and the John Stuart Mill of the *Principles of Political Economy* (1848)—he later moved over to a Cobdenite position—who were not anti-imperialist, but advocates of magnificent programmes of colonization and the formulators of doctrines of what might be called an 'informal' empire of free trade. Their devotion to empire rested substantially upon their view that only in this way could an industrial Britain, with ever increasing productive and capital resources, keep its factories busy, its workmen employed, and ward off the dangers of crisis and possible civil war. The view of these economists had been in decided contrast with those of the so-called Manchester School, of Richard Cobden and his able lieutenant, John Bright. Cobden and Bright were devotees of *laissez-faire*—their Benthamite economist brethren often saw pressing reasons for governmental intervention—and cosmopolitans, preaching the ideal of a free international economy in which colonies would be a burden rather than a benefit. The non-Cobdenite Liberals, on the other hand, supported the Jamaica Committee in order to strengthen the empire.

By the 1860's, most advanced Liberal opinion had passed over from the pro-colonial views of the Radical economists to the anti-colonialism of the Cobdenites. The former point of view, however, was still set forth by the weekly *Economist*, in an article, on 9th December 1865. While agreeing with Eyre's supporters that the Empire was a great asset, the *Economist* did not agree that the methods of Governor Eyre would prove most useful to its maintenance. That journal's view that the policy of justice to the darker races would prove much more useful was in conformity with the increasing tendency of British capital to seek investment opportunities outside the bounds of the 'formal' Empire. A forerunner, perhaps, of a later Liberal-Imperialism, the Liberal weekly pictured a vast empire in which the coloured races would work under British management and with British technical assistance to bring railroads and industry to the undeveloped parts of the globe. To achieve this goal, it was necessary, the journal believed, for Great Britain to establish a reputation for treating the coloured races fairly. Methods such as Eyre had employed in Jamaica would hardly give England a good name, nor, of course, could such methods succeed in getting loyal and effective work from the native races. Therefore, the *Economist* concluded, Eyre had to be severely reprimanded. Exeter Hall and Frederic Harrison might wish to have justice for the coloured races because injustice in Jamaica would make injustice easier in England. The *Economist* had the additional reason that such justice was in the long-range interest of the British Empire.

7

THE PROSECUTION

The first of the 'Jamaica Prosecutions,' during the last months of 1866 and the early months of 1867 at Kingston, received little attention in England. A sadistic Provost Marshal, Ramsay, who, during the suppression, had spent from early morning to late evening flogging or supervising the flogging of Negroes, had been turned over to the civil courts but a Jamaica grand jury had refused to indict. Another civil officer, Woodrow, had shown a perverted fondness for flogging women prisoners; he too was cleared by a Jamaica grand jury. Since a fair trial could not be obtained on the island, there had been some speculation in the Colonial Office about bringing Ramsay and Woodrow, as well as other offenders, to England for their trials. But, since the prosecution had been hanging over their heads for so long, the decision had been against this; it was believed 'that it would be against the spirit of British Criminal jurisprudence to do so,' as a cabinet spokesman told the House of Commons. Such an action, he added, would also have the unhappy effect of keeping the Jamaica agitation alive. Two servicemen, Ensign Cullen and Surgeon Morris, were charged with putting Negroes to death without trial, and officers were sent from England to hear their cases. After the fullest hearings, from October 1866 through February 1867, both were acquitted, as 'impartial' service courts martial arrived at the same verdict as highly prejudiced Jamaica grand juries.

The Admiralty announced that the participation of naval personnel at the Morant Bay courts martial 'was deserving of disapprobation,' but decided to forget the entire business since the officers had been young and inexperienced and, in the majority of cases, the proceedings had been confirmed by superior officers.

One of these young naval officers—Lieutenant Herbert Brand—had achieved early notoriety because of his service as the President of the court martial board which had sentenced Gordon to be hung. After Brand's conduct had been denounced in Parliament by Charles Buxton in July 1866, the lieutenant had addressed a letter to Buxton, part of which read:

> You may be a very fine *buckra*[1] among the polished gentlemen at Exeter Hall who wanted Mr Eyre suspended with a rope, and the old ladies of Clapham; but when you come with your peculiar little assertions in print, and such barefaced lies, too, I think it is time for the trampled worm to turn.

It was thought intolerable that a junior officer of the navy should be permitted to address a member of parliament in such terms, and Brand was suspended and placed upon half-pay. Colonel Alexander Abercrombie Nelson was another object of concentrated fire. His role in confirming the sentence of death upon Gordon was central, but all his actions as commander-in-chief of the military forces at Morant Bay were at issue. The Jamaica Committee could not forget Governor Eyre's original dispatch in which he had praised Nelson's services, and had added that 'we never had a difference of opinion, even upon the propriety or policy of a single act or movement.' The legal action which was being prepared in England was to devolve exclusively upon Governor Eyre, Colonel Nelson, and Lieutenant Brand.

Legal preparations had been long in the making. As early as January 1866, the Jamaica Committee had con-

[1] A term for 'white man' employed by the Jamaican Negroes.

sulted two well-known barristers as to the proper manner
of invoking the law in the case of Governor Eyre. One of
them, James Fitzjames Stephen, whose grandfather had
been one of the stalwarts of the anti-slavery campaign, and
whose father, a former permanent under-secretary of the
colonial office, had had many brushes with the Jamaica
planters, had an 'inherited' interest in the case. It was he
who drew up an opinion which held that Eyre, most especially in the case of Gordon, was guilty of what was,
technically, murder. The Jamaica Committee had selected
Shaen and Roscoe as its solicitors, a well-known firm which
in the 'sixties and for many years afterwards acted as the
attorneys of leading British trade unions. William Shaen was
personally active in many Radical causes. In October 1866,
the Jamaica Committee requested its solicitors to proceed
in obtaining indictments.

On the 5th of February, 1867, the day when the
second session of the parliament elected in July of 1865
was opened by the Queen, a leading article in *The Times*
announced that 'a new act in the Jamaica tragedy' was
about to begin. 'The step long threatened by the Jamaica
Committee has at last been taken,' the paper continued.
The first moves in the prosecution of Colonel Nelson and
Lieutenant Herbert Brand had been made: applications
for warrants had been filed at the Bow-Street Police Court
by Fitzjames Stephen. The charge was wilful murder.
Stephen informed Sir Thomas Henry, the Chief Magistrate at Bow Street, that he would have moved for a warrant against Governor Eyre as well, but that that gentleman was not at the time within the jurisdiction of the Bow
Street court. Hearings began on the following day.

'Sir,' Stephen began in addressing the court, 'it is one of
the leading peculiarities, perhaps the greatest peculiarity,
of the English law, that it can be set in motion by any
private person who considers that those in whom he takes
an interest have been wronged, or that the interests of the
public require that criminal proceedings should be instituted.' 'So when a great wrong is committed,' Stephen
continued, 'and a precedent seems to be about to be set

up, which, if allowed to stand, would put in peril the lives and liberties of other persons in the British Empire, in these islands as well as elsewhere, it is not merely the right but the duty of those who regard such precedents with apprehension, to use those means with which they are by law intrusted, and bring the matter before a court of law, by which it may be determined whether their view is correct or not.' The private prosecutors in this case, John Stuart Mill, M.P. for Westminister, and P. A. Taylor, M.P. for Leicester, wished English judges and juries to determine what was and what was not lawful behaviour. The murdered man, for whose murderers the prosecutors were now seeking warrants, was George William Gordon. The key legal question, barrister Stephen concluded, was whether law was to be paramount within the British Empire, or whether the Queen or her officers could, at will, set aside the law and establish a military despotism with the power of life and death.

Two Negro Jamaicans, brought over to England by the Jamaica Committee, gave evidence, as required by law, to prove that a crime had actually been committed. The following day, Sir Thomas Henry, after considering the facts, issued warrants for the arrest of both officers. Stephen had made a point of requesting that the warrant be served in such a fashion that the defendants would not suffer the slightest disrespect or loss of personal dignity, also urging that they not be held in custody, but be admitted to bail. Stephen's motive was obvious: to have treated Brand and Nelson as common criminals would have brought the public to sympathize with them even more than already was the case. Yet, as Sir Thomas Henry remarked, when the charge was murder, the granting of bail was highly unusual. On Saturday morning, the 9th of February, Lieutenant Brand was brought to court to hear the charges against him, and was released on his own recognizances of £500, and two sureties of £200 each. A little later that same day, Colonel Alexander Nelson surrendered himself to the court and was bound over under the same conditions.

On the following Monday, February 11th, two days after
Nelson and Brand had surrendered to the court and been
released on bail, there was another Reform demonstration
in Trafalgar Square. The winter sun was shining brightly
and the weather was unseasonably mild. The Reform
League officials had called for good order along the line
of march and had asked the marchers to keep silent while
passing the clubs along St James and Pall Mall, on their
way to the Agricultural Hall, where an evening meeting
was to take place. On the balcony of the Athenaeum, the
Archbishop of York chatted with Charles Dickens as they
watched the long procession of workingmen. Opposite the
Athenaeum, at the United Service Club—the club to which
Colonel Nelson belonged—the Prince of Wales and the
Duke of Edinburgh watched the crowds. At the Agricultural Hall, at about seven o'clock that evening, the
President of the League, Edmond Beales, took the platform
and read a letter from John Stuart Mill to the assemblage.
Among the evening's speakers were Professor Thorold
Rogers, T. B. Potter, M.P., P. A. Taylor, M.P., and Professor Beesly—all Jamaica Committee stalwarts. Two days
after the Reform demonstration, on Wednesday, February
13th, about 800 Fenians sacked a coast-guard station in
County Kerry, seizing arms, shooting a mounted police-
man, and cutting telegraph wires. Other Fenians, believed
to have come from New York, were apprehended just as
they were about to launch an attack on Chester Castle in
order to seize the arms stored there.

Both domestic and imperial disorder were much in the
public mind when the inquiry into the cases of Nelson
and Brand resumed on Tuesday morning, February 12th,
in a crowded courtroom. Many who had come too late
could not be admitted. The solicitor for the Admiralty
appeared for Lieutenant Brand and the solicitor for the
War Office represented Colonel Nelson. That this was so,
was the result of the parliamentary efforts of supporters of
Governor Eyre, who felt—with some reason—that if Nelson
and Brand were to be placed in jeopardy of their lives,
since the charge was murder, for carrying out the orders

of their superiors, the government was obliged to defend
them. In a lengthy address, opening the case for the prosecution, barrister Stephen declared that his intention was
to have the courts determine whether Gordon had been
properly executed. Since his purpose was a 'technical' one,
Stephen announced that he was going to treat the accused
not as murderers, but as gentlemen. The question involved
martial law. Martial law could only be legally employed
when used to suppress a revolt; when used to punish a
crime, it was illegal: when Nelson had postponed Gordon's
execution until after the Sabbath, stating, at the time, that
his immediate execution was not essential to the safety of
that part of the island, the Colonel had virtually admitted
that Gordon had been hanged because he was 'an agitator,'
and not because his execution was necessary to put a halt
to the insurrection. In English law, there was no other
name for such an act than 'wilful murder,' Stephen concluded. When the defendants left the courtroom that
day and stepped into their cabs, a crowd which had
gathered outside the courthouse broke into loud cheers
for the 'persecuted men.' When the hearings resumed
over a week later, the solicitors assigned to the defendants
by the government presented their case: the defendants,
they argued, had simply been obeying orders, and, if they
had declined to obey them, they would themselves have
been liable to be executed. Under such circumstances,
could they be held personally accountable? The War Office solicitor called the pre-trial examination a 'solemn and
serious farce,' simply a preparation for the trial not of the
present defendants but of Governor Eyre. Stephen, in reply, asserted that the orders had been illegal and that if
the defendants had refused to obey them and had been
court martialed for their refusal, they would certainly have
been exonerated, demonstrating that his faith in the justice
of court martial procedure remained unimpaired by the
events at Morant Bay. Sir Thomas Henry listened carefully
to all the arguments, quietly interjecting a question here
and there, and, deciding that the case warranted further
inquiry, sent it on to the Central Criminal Court.

Ex-Governor Eyre had not attended these preliminary hearings, in the prosecution of Nelson and Brand. According to his friends, he had most chivalrously determined to come to London to stand by his officers. But, since this would have placed him within the jurisdiction of the courts of London and exposed him to prosecution, his supporters had persuaded him to give up his purpose. It had been most difficult to hold him back, but, as Anderson Rose, Eyre's solicitor, explained to the press, 'sound sense dictates that he should not voluntarily attend to be prosecuted.'

Eyre was living at Adderley Hall, in Shropshire, at this time—and the Jamaica Committee, through its solicitors, Shaen and Roscoe, followed him there. Shropshire, a Welsh border county of green fields, unclouded by London's smoke and fog, was a bit of the older England, still free from the bustle of the widening influence of the metropolis. But now the controversies of London were reaching out. In the rural counties, justice was dispensed not by 'professional' judges, but by the well-to-do gentlemen Justices of the Peace. It was to persuade such a group of gentlemen-justices that Shaen and Roscoe repaired, on 25th March 1867, to the magistrates of the Market Drayton Petty Sessional Division, to request a warrant for the arrest of Edward Eyre as an accessory before the fact in the murder of George William Gordon.

The courtroom was unusually crowded. The ladies and gentlemen of the district were decidedly interested in this prosecution of their new neighbour. For the past several days, the people of Market Drayton and of the surrounding countryside had talked of little else, and now as many of the townspeople as could had come. From little expressions of sentiment, it was clear that the sympathies of the local people were entirely with Eyre. There was a full attendance of magistrates as well. Before the matter could proceed, two of the local justices felt compelled to disqualify themselves from hearing the case on grounds that they had contributed to the Eyre Defence Fund and felt themselves strongly prejudiced. It was not unlikely that the non-contributing justices shared the views of their more open-pursed colleagues. Fitzjames Stephen, who had journeyed from London to address the Petty Sessions, launched into a recital of the history of the Jamaica Affair, but was curtly cut short by the chairman of the Shropshire justices who considered the story irrelevant. After much wrangling, the magistrates reluctantly agreed to issue a warrant requiring Eyre's presence when the hearings resumed.

On the 27th of March, two days later, the hearings resumed, and Eyre himself was present. Once again the courtroom was crowded. This time the curious townspeople were joined by the prominent landowners of the neighbourhood, and some of these gentlemen sat themselves beside the Governor in the courtroom as an indication of their faith in his integrity. The gentlemen-magistrates vainly attempted to maintain judicial calm despite their obvious sympathies, and listened uncomfortably as Fitzjames Stephen, continuing the tactic he had employed in London of treating the defendant with such courtesy and respect that it ill-fitted the charge, made his presentations. The Eyre Defence Committee had engaged as the Governor's barrister Hardinge Stanley Giffard, who smiled affably and had chatted contentedly with the magistrates before the hearing had begun. Giffard, a short, stout man, was in 1866 still at the beginning of a career, which was to take him by 1885, as the Earl of Halsbury, to the post of Lord Chancellor, and by 1910, to the leadership of the 'die hard' faction of the House of Lords. In later years, Giffard regarded his handling of the Eyre case, through its successive stages, as the greatest triumph of his career at the bar.

Giffard's opening speech was directed at the emotions and prejudices of the country gentlemen who heard it, and its dramatic, even theatrical quality was admirably suited to the occasion. It lasted six full hours. Giffard depicted the tortured thoughts which must have run through the mind of the defendant when he had first heard of the start of the insurrection—the fears of men killed and mutilated, of women raped and children gutted—and he described, not without a peculiar relish, atrocities actually perpetrated in years past at Santo Domingo and Haiti. The justices listened intently to the expertly-told tales. How could Eyre be sure that these horrors would not occur in Jamaica, Giffard asked the court? He reminded the justices of an expression used by Gordon: 'You must do as they did in Haiti.' Was this not enough to chill the blood? Yet Eyre was being criticized because, 'Having *that* before him, and having the lives and honour of all those whom his Queen had sent him to protect at the moment dependent upon his promptitude, it was now said: "You formed a rash judgment. You ought not to have done it. We will hunt and persecute you to death!"' 'Good God!' Giffard shouted, his eyes welling up with tears. 'Is that Justice?'

The result was inevitable. The magistrates consulted briefly and unanimously discharged Eyre. The evidence presented by the prosecutors, the Shropshire justices declared, did not raise a strong or a probable presumption of guilt. The supporters of Governor Eyre were delighted and his opponents outraged by the news from Shropshire. When Eyre's discharge became known in Market Drayton, the bells of the local Anglican Church were tolled in triumph. Then—with a kind of miraculous spontaneity— churches in neighbouring Shropshire villages also rang their bells, and even in London, church bells joyously sounded in celebration. Justice had been done in the case of that valiant and loyal son of the Church of England, Edward John Eyre! 'Respectable' men throughout Great Britain rejoiced in his triumph—in the triumph of order. *Punch*, that piping voice of the English middle classes, gave vent to its emotions in a breathless bit entitled, 'Free as Eyre':

Well done, old Shropshire! Well done, Market Drayton! Quite right to ring the bells when the sensible Salopian Magistrates apprised Mr Peter Taylor that he might go back to Town and inform Mr Beales (M.A.), MR SHAMMYRUMSTUFF, and their tail, that there was no evidence on which GOVERNOR EYRE could properly be committed. . . . English good sense is seldom appealed

to in vain. We really cannot murder a man for saving
a colony. It may be, theoretically, proper to kill him,
but the fact that Jamaica now belongs to the QUEEN of
ENGLAND, and not to the 'brown-skinned, canting, dis-
reputable agitator,' GORDON, is a fact which somewhat
overrides theories. . . . Some manifestation of English
sympathy with a persecuted officer must be made.
Meantime, why not return MR EYRE for Middlesex?

The supporters of the Jamaica Committee, on the other
hand, thought the decision of the Shropshire magistrates
less attributable to good sense than to class prejudice.
Edmond Beales, the president of the Reform League, made
a public declaration that Eyre would be punished if the
whole Reform League had to become his prosecutors. He
asserted that the 'democratic' cause—the cause of the
Reform League—had received a setback with the exon-
eration of Eyre. A pro-Eyre paper suggested, when commenting on Beale's statement, that 'the connection between Mr Eyre and Reform may be as difficult to discover
as the connection between Mr Beales and good sense.'
Many pro-Eyre journals were angry at the courteous
treatment which the Governor had received at the hands
of Stephen. Since they had pictured the prosecution of Eyre
in melodramatic terms, they were disappointed that
Stephen had not behaved sufficiently 'vindictively.' An
editorial in *The Times* read:

We cannot but think that when so odious an accusation
is brought forward, all compliments and expressions of
sympathy on the part of prosecuting counsel are entirely out of place. The defendant can as little desire to
receive the ghastly courtesy as the prosecutors, if they
really believe in his guilt, can be sincere in offering it.

A few days later, *The Times* published a reply to its
hostile article from barrister Stephen, who noted that the
chairman of the Shropshire magistrates had, in fact, re-
proved him for his 'abuse of Mr Eyre' in the courtroom.
'It is easy to treat Mr Eyre as a spotless hero or as a

cowardly murderer,' Stephen wrote. 'It is not so easy to show how, without being either the one or the other, he came to commit one of the score of dissimilar actions which the law of England calls murder for one of the score of dissimilar motives which the law of England calls express malice.' The barrister concluded by stating that he had 'treated Mr Eyre precisely as I have often treated the most obscene[1] and uninteresting criminals.'

In the last of his letters to the *Daily News*, Frederic Harrison had reported the views of those who believed that if the case reached a grand jury, the jury would ignore the bill of indictment. Grand juries were chosen from wealthier and therefore, presumably, more socially responsible classes, and they, it was felt, could be relied upon to support 'order.' This judgment was soon to be tested. On Wednesday, 10th April 1867, the charge in the cases of Nelson and Brand was read to the Middlesex grand jury which was to determine whether Colonel Nelson and Lieutenant Brand were to be indicted and placed upon trial for the murder of George William Gordon. The charge was to be read by the Lord Chief Justice of England, Sir Alexander Cockburn, the highest judicial officer under the British constitution, barring only the Lord Chancellor. When Cockburn decided that he would take upon himself the task of preparing and delivering the charge, the interest of the London press quickened. In a way, a half-way shrewd journalist or barrister might have guessed that he would take the opportunity to enter the case, for Cockburn—unlike many of his more scholarly judicial colleagues—liked a good show and, in the past, had frequently insisted upon trying the most sensational cases. The 'charge', the statement of the law as it per-

[1] The following day, Stephen, 'with many apologies for my bad handwriting', explained that he had written 'obscure' rather than 'obscene'. The gentlemanly *Times*—feeling, no doubt, that it had at last unmasked the prosecutor for the villain he was—tartly replied that 'there can be no doubt that the word as written in the m.s. now before us is "obscene".'

tained to the case, frequently included a recommendation
to the grand jury. In effect, the charging justice could
direct the grand jury to bring in a 'true bill,' that is a
formal indictment, or 'No true bill,' in which event the
case would be thrown out of court. The grand jury was not
obliged to accept the judge's advice, but it usually did so.
In the days preceding the 10th, there were rumours that
Cockburn was hard at work. The Lord Chief Justice's
previous charges had been much admired—some of his
charges and judgments, indeed, were regarded as master-
pieces of legal style, although even steadfast admirers
admitted that subordinate justices might have a more profound knowledge of the law.

Cockburn was a Palmerstonian Liberal, not a Radical,
who, in the 'thirties and 'forties had made his reputation
as a barrister, and, in 1847, had been elected a Liberal
Member of Parliament. As a result of a parliamentary
defence of Palmerston, when the old man had been hard-
pressed during the Don Pacifico affair, Cockburn had been
knighted and made solicitor-general, and, early in 1848,
had been advanced to the position of Attorney-General.
In 1856, Cockburn was named Chief Justice of the Court
of Common Pleas and in 1859, Palmerston had had him
named Lord Chief Justice of England. A short, square man
of military bearing, Cockburn had the highest regard for
the dignity of his office and rarely omitted the elaborate
ceremonials attached to it. On the day of the reading of
the charge, he arrived at the Sessions House in the Old
Bailey at about 10 A.M., fully dressed in his magnificent
robes of state, there to be greeted by the Lord Mayor,
the Sheriff and Under-Sheriffs of London, all fully robed.
This splendid entourage was escorted amid great pomp
to the court by eight aldermen of the City of London.
When the procession arrived, the courtroom was already
crowded. Newspaper reporters were ready to take short-
hand notes of the charge. The noted Whig, Earl Granville,
who had been the Lord President of the Council in the
Russell government of 1866, was present and seated himself beside the Lord Mayor. The bustling courtroom, with
its distinguished assemblage, the ornate robes, the stately

ceremonies, all contributed to the impression, as one journal put it 'of a state trial'. It was difficult to remember that the state—at least the War Office and the Admiralty—was on the side of the defence rather than of the prosecution. The first order of business—just as at the Market Drayton hearings—was an announcement by the jury's foreman that one of the jurors had been compelled to absent himself because he had formed such strong views on the question. It later developed that he was a clerk in the War Office.

The Lord Chief Justice of England began reading his charge at about 10:15 A.M. He continued, without an interruption, until a few minutes after four in the afternoon. It was a herculean performance, almost unknown at the time, although in a case some years later Cockburn was to outdo himself in a charge which lasted eighteen days and which, when published, filled two volumes of 800 pages each. In his lengthy charge, Cockburn painstakingly traced the tragic details of the incidents at Morant Bay, discussed the applicabilities of the martial and the common law, and, in the most scholarly fashion, outlined the historical and judicial precedents. It was to the question of martial law that he gave his most pressing attention, and it was plain from the first that his views on the subject were little different from those of Frederic Harrison. Had the Governor of Jamaica, Cockburn inquired, the power to proclaim martial law because he exercised the prerogative of the Crown? In a Crown Colony, certainly, the power of the executive was absolute, but Jamaica had become a 'settled' colony under Charles II, the justice continued, and the English colonists had brought with them the Common Law of England. If, under circumstances of rebellion, martial law could be declared in Jamaica, why then it could as readily be declared in England itself. Armed rebels who had been captured in the course of suppressing a rebellion might, of course, be put to death without any trial whatsoever. But, even under such circumstances, some lingering doubts would remain as to the state of the law, for, in the reign of Richard II, when the rebels who had followed Wat Tyler had been executed without a trial, it was thought necessary to pass an Act of Indemnity to exempt their executors from punishment. And so the Lord Chief Justice described precedent after precedent. Cockburn's final conclusion: the law of England knew no such thing as 'martial law.' Parliament, in 1628, had passed the Petition of Right which had declared all commissions for trial of British subjects by martial law illegal. That act of parliament had never been repealed, the judge reminded the grand jury, and since the passage of that act, no sovereign had dared to proclaim martial law in Great Britain. Cockburn admitted that it had been proclaimed in Ireland during the rebellion of 1798. Wolfe Tone, the leader of the Irish rebellion, had been tried by court martial and had been sentenced to hang. But, on application, the Court of King's Bench had granted a writ of *habeas corpus* and had asserted that Tone was amenable only to the civil courts. Martial law was military law, Cockburn concluded, law which could be applied only to the armed services; the right to put down rebellion was derived not from the martial but from the common law.

The Lord Chief Justice next turned his attention to the specific facts of the case before him. 'I suppose,' he began, 'there is no island or place in the world, in which there has been so much of insurrection and disorder as the island of Jamaica. There is no place in which the curse which attaches to slavery, both as regards the master and the slave, has been more strikingly illustrated.' Cockburn described the illegality of the seizure of Gordon at Kingston and his subsequent transportation to Morant Bay, and posed many technical objections to Gordon's trial. He summed up his view in biting phrases:

After the most careful perusal of the evidence which was adduced against him, I come irresistibly to the conclusion that if a man had been tried upon that evidence —I must correct myself. He could not have been tried upon that evidence. No competent judge acquainted with the duties of his office could have received that evidence. Three-fourths, I had almost said nine-tenths, of the evidence upon which that man was convicted and sentenced to death, was evidence which, according to no known rules—not only of ordinary law, but of military law—according to no rules of right or justice, could possibly have been admitted; and it never would have been admitted if a competent judge had presided, or if there had been the advantage of a military officer of any experience in the practice of courts martial.

The Lord Chief Justice concluded by urging the jurors not to allow opinions formed during the widespread public discussion of the case to influence them. 'Passion and prejudice should never, under any circumstances, be allowed to enter into the arcana of justice,' he warned. The Grand Jury then withdrew from the courtroom.

The charge of the Chief Justice had come as something of a surprise to the jurymen as well as to the public at large. Cockburn—despite his Palmerstonian past—had, in effect, asked for an indictment. The jury returned to the court on the following morning and considered the case from about ten o'clock until half-past one—a comparatively short time given the complexity of the issues. When they returned to the courtroom, the jury's foreman reported agreement in finding 'no bill' in the cases of both Colonel Nelson and Lieutenant Brand. The jury had decided to ignore the Lord Chief Justice and the case was to be thrown out of court. Members of the Bar who happened to be present in the court that day broke into applause when they heard the decision. The jury's last word was a suggestion, which it urged to be given to the proper authorities, that 'martial law should be more clearly defined by legislative enactment.'

The day following the verdict, *The Times* commented editorially on the 'just' presentation of the charge made by the Lord Chief Justice; the paper regarded Cockburn's charge as 'unflinching in its vindication of the law, and conspicuous for its assertion of moral right' and 'equally merciful towards the defendants.' Yet *The Times* was also quite pleased with the grand jury's decision which had

put an end to this 'ill-advised prosecution.' 'The failure of
the indictment is equivalent to an amnesty for the past,'
the paper concluded, and 'the emphatic protest of the
Chief Justice will remain on record as a warning for the
future.'

The immediate reaction of the English public was much
like that of *The Times*. The verdict was one which the
great majority of the public desired—and there was no
further need to cavil about the charge. Members of the
bench, and especially high members of the bench, enjoyed
great prestige in Great Britain. Up until the point when
the Lord Chief Justice had declared what the law was,
there had been controversy on legal subtleties. After the
delivery of Cockburn's charge, many pro-Eyre newspapers
and much of the public had changed their tune. The Lord
Chief Justice had spoken, and that was the law. That did
not mean that the supporters of Governor Eyre had come
around to accepting the views of the Jamaica Committee.
Not at all. The public, like *The Times*, and the Grand
Jury, had simply divided the Jamaica business into sep-
arate compartments. They were willing to accept Cockburn's constitutional views concerning martial law, but at
the same time insisted upon judging Colonel Nelson and
Lieutenant Brand not guilty of murder.

Despite the verdict of the Grand Jury, the Radical papers
exulted in triumph. The charge of the Lord Chief Justice
had confirmed their view of the law. The *Spectator* threw
this bouquet at the Jamaica Committee:

> We can scarcely doubt that, for the future, no one will
> venture to depreciate the service achieved by the
> Jamaica Committee in eliciting from the Chief Justice
> of England the masterly and luminous statement.

Commenting on the effect upon public opinion which the
charge had had, the paper added that 'Nobody else would
have had a tithe of that influence, not the Primate, not the
Premier, not the greatest thinker in the kingdom.' It was
some time before the full significance of Cockburn's charge
was widely understood—as the Liberal *Spectator* under-

stood it. If the Lord Chief Justice were correct and martial law was unknown to the law of England, how could Great Britain maintain order in its empire, say, in Ireland, where Fenian outbreaks were becoming increasingly more dangerous?

In the early summer, the Cockburn opinion was debated in the House of Commons. An Irish member for Longford Co., M. W. O'Reilly, rose in the House on 2nd July 1867, to offer a resolution. He quoted that part of the charge which had stated that no British citizen could be subjected to martial law. To an Irishman like himself, O'Reilly declared, the Chief Justice's charge had had 'a vital and a thrilling interest.' The subject of martial law, he told the house, 'might be a subject of abstract theory in England, but in Ireland and the colonies it was a matter of vital importance that there should be no ambiguity.' O'Reilly proposed that 'this House would regard as utterly void and illegal any commission or proclamation purporting or pretending to proclaim Martial Law in any part of this Kingdom.' He was supported by a lengthy speech by W. E. Forster, for on the theoretical issue of martial law most Liberals united behind Cockburn's charge. Speaking of the events in Jamaica, Forster declared that 'our honour, our position as a country, and, more than all, our duty, should lead us to say that such things must not happen again.' Gathorne Hardy, the Tory Home Secretary, however, defended the use of martial law at times of insurrection, adding that the O'Reilly resolution, if passed, would 'hang *in terrorem* over the heads' of any government. He reminded the house that the Chief Justice's views had been, after all, a charge and not a judicial decision. At the same time, however, he calmed O'Reilly's fears for Ireland and assured him that the government had no intention of declaring martial law, but he begged the House 'not to place an impediment in the way of those who were acting in distant spheres, and to whom, with great responsibilities, was committed the duty of upholding the authority of the Crown and the rights of the country.' In this he was supported by Edward Cardwell, the former Liberal Colonial Secretary, who urged O'Reilly to withdraw his resolution.

O'Reilly agreed not to proceed further and the government's formal right to employ martial law, even in the United Kingdom, was left unassailed by the House.

There was a debate in the House of Lords about the charge some two weeks after its discussion in the Commons. The distaste for the Chief Justice proved keen among peers such as Lord Denman, who reminded the House that the grand jury had obviously not thought very much of the charge since it had thrown out the indictment, and Viscount Melville, a long-time defender of Eyre, who added, for his part, that 'a more unjust, unfair, and partial charge never was delivered by any Judge from the Bench.' But Chelmsford, the Lord Chancellor, gallantly defended Cockburn against the assault, stating that 'it was impossible to do ample justice to the research and the ability which that Charge displays.'

The harshest words about Sir Alexander Cockburn and his charge were written by the incorrigible Carlyle. Readers of his *Shooting Niagara: And After?*, a sermon against granting the vote to the workingman, will remember the celebrated passage in which he flayed the Lord Chief Justice:

We have also our remarkable 'Jamaica Committee'; and a Lord Chief Justice 'speaking six hours' (with such 'eloquence,' such etc. etc. as takes with ravishment the general Editorial ear, Penny and Three-penny), to prove that there is no such thing or ever was as Martial Law—and that any governor, commanded soldier, or official person, putting down the frightfulest Mob-insurrection, Black or White, shall do it with a rope round *his* neck, by way of encouragement to him. Nobody answers this remarkable Lord Chief Justice, 'Lordship, if you were to speak for six hundred years, instead of six hours, you would only prove the more to us that, unwritten if you will, but real and fundamental, anterior to all written laws and first making written laws *possible*, there must have been, and is, and will be, coeval with Human Society from its very beginnings to its ultimate end, an actual *Martial Law*, of more validity than any other law whatever. Lordship, if there is no written law that three and three shall be six, do you wonder at the Statute Book for that omission? You may shut those eloquent lips and go home to dinner. May your shadow never be less; greater it perhaps has little chance of being.

Later in this sermon, Carlyle once again denounced the 'rabid Nigger Philanthropists' of the Jamaica Committee, and concluded that he now lived in a country where it was thought 'safer to humour the mob than repress them, with the rope about *your* neck.'

After the disappointment of Market Drayton and the failure of the grand jury to indict Nelson and Brand, Fitzjames Stephen advised the leaders of the Jamaica Committee to drop its case against Eyre, cautioning them that no further good could come of continuing the prosecution, that to go on would make it appear that the Committee was vindictively persecuting the Governor. He found his advice most unwelcome. For some time now, John Stuart Mill had been unhappy with Stephen's legal services. The two men —Stephen and Mill—were thoroughly incompatible. Stephen was a faithful follower of Mill in many matters, but on certain others—on the issue of democracy, for example —the barrister felt himself closer to his good friend Carlyle. Furthermore, Stephen found Carlyle personally more attractive than the passionless, calculating machine he thought Mill to be; the 'passionless' Mill, on his side, found Stephen not sufficiently enthusiastic in his handling of the Eyre prosecution. This failing had appeared quite markedly when contrasted with Giffard's fervent eloquence at Market Drayton. Mill was determined to continue the prosecution and easily persuaded the most prominent members of the Jamaica Committee's executive that the Committee ought to persist in its efforts. Under these circumstances, Stephen was dropped as the Committee's barrister.

The Eyre group had a unity of purpose which the Jamaica Committee lacked in late 1867 and early 1868.

Lindsley Aspland, for example, one of the members of the Committee's executive, told his colleagues that, since the Shropshire magistrates had refused to take any action against Eyre, the ex-Governor should be left in contempt. After all, Aspland said, Chief Justice Cockburn had already proclaimed the constitutional doctrine which the Jamaica Committee had wished to assert. Supported by others on the Committee, Aspland argued in this fashion throughout the last half of 1867 and the early weeks of 1868. However, the top leadership of the Jamaica Committee—men like Mill, Taylor, Hughes, Huxley, Miall, and Bright—refused to budge. They would persevere in their intention of bringing the case of Edward Eyre before a British jury. Finally Aspland, as had Buxton before him, decided to withdraw. When he wrote Mill to this effect, the chairman expressed his regrets at Aspland's decision and made this reply to his arguments:

> You talk of leaving Eyre to contempt. What he would be left to is boastful triumph, followed by the fruits of victory in the shape of lucrative Government employment, probably with the power to do again what he has done, and with undiminished if not increased disposition to do it.
>
> This is not like a contest for some political improvement, in which the only question is whether it shall be obtained a little sooner or a little later. Ours is, morally, a protest against a series of atrocious crimes, and politically an assertion of the authority of the criminal law over public delinquents. This protest and vindication must be made now or never.

But the position of the Jamaica Committee had not been entirely unaffected by its two failures. The Committee gave up its plan to prosecute Governor Eyre for murder. Belatedly, Mill had come around to the position which had been taken the preceding year by Charles Buxton. After the jury had failed to act in the Nelson and Brand case, Mill had become convinced that it would be all but impossible to obtain an indictment for murder against Edward Eyre. The Jamaica Committee's new tactic would be to seek an indictment against the ex-Governor for 'high crimes and misdemeanours' as they had been defined under the Colonial Governors Act. The day after the Middlesex grand jury had announced its verdict, the Jamaica Committee informed the press and the public of its new intention.

Governor Eyre had been away on a short trip during the presentation of the Lord Chief Justice's charge and the subsequent deliberations of the grand jury. When he returned to Adderley Hall, he found a letter from his solicitor waiting for him; it informed him of the Jamaica Committee's intention to continue the prosecution, although on altered grounds. A few days after his return, Eyre wrote his barrister, Hardinge Giffard:

> . . . What a very satisfactory confirmation of the views of the Market Drayton justices was the action of the Grand Jury in Nelson's and Brand's cases—in spite of the violent and partisan charge of Sir A. Cockburn! You will have seen it formally announced that the Jamaica Committee now intend to proceed against me under the Governor's Act for misdemeanour. . . .
>
> I confess I do not like being left to the tender mercies of Chief Justice Cockburn . . . and after the specimen we had of his bias in his charge to the Criminal Court Grand Jury, it is quite clear he would do all in his power or beyond it, to further the end or object of the Jamaica Committee.
>
> . . . Whatever the Jamaica ctee. (sic) intend to attempt, I hope they will do it at once, as I am anxious to have the whole matter settled one way or the other. It has been in progress for more than twelve months, and this continued suspense, anxiety and annoyance is telling sadly upon Mrs Eyre. . . .

On the 22nd of May 1867, the Derby was run. Sleet had showered upon the track before the race. Consequently the winner that day was not the favourite, but the muddy track proved to be just right for a horse named Hermit.

Before the race, those 'in the know' had referred to him
disparagingly as 'poor Hermit.' The odds? 100 to 1. No
known odds are known to have been set by bookmakers
on the chances of Mill and his colleagues procuring an
indictment against the former Governor of Jamaica. If they
had been, they might have been fixed at 100 to 1 against
a grand jury finding a 'true bill' against Edward Eyre. But
Hermit, 'poor Hermit,' had made it—and who knew?

In January 1868, the case of Edward Eyre took a new
turn. The ex-Governor had moved his residence from
Shropshire to London, placing himself within the jurisdiction of the courts of Middlesex. With a touch of bravado,
he requested his solicitor to write to the Jamaica Committee to inform it of his new address, a blunt challenge
designed to answer the accusations of cowardice which
had been hurled at him when he chose to remain in Shropshire during the trial of Nelson and Brand. Eyre was tired
of having the prosecution hanging over his head. He
wished it to come and be finally over with.

On February 27th, Sir Robert Collier, the barrister
whom the Committee had engaged after its sacking of
Fitzjames Stephen, came before Sir Thomas Henry in the
Bow Street Court to apply for a warrant against Eyre. The
charge was murder—the Jamaica Committee had, at the
last minute, determined to make one further attempt to
secure the indictment of Eyre upon this charge. The barrister urged Sir Thomas not to be influenced by the course
adopted by the Shropshire magistrates, 'country justices'
who had no knowledge of the law and whose decision had
been reached before the delivery of the now famous
charge of the Lord Chief Justice. After brief consideration,
Chief Magistrate Henry denied Sir Robert's request, ruling
that the crime for which Collier was now seeking an arrest
warrant had also been involved in the case against Nelson
and Brand, and since the grand jury in that case had found
no grounds for indictment, it was pointless to re-try it.

Eyre's supporters in the press were jubilant. The leading
article of *The Times* exulted in Sir Thomas Henry's decision, and congratulated itself on having finally heard the
'last' of Governor Eyre and of the Jamaica Committee.

'That Mr Eyre acted unadvisedly may be admitted,' the paper asserted; 'that he was unable to free himself from the contagion of local terrors and the vehemence of local feeling is plain.' 'For these, which are political offences, he has been judged and has suffered.' 'Those who would make Mr Eyre a murderer,' the paper continued, 'provoke those who would make him a hero, and both classes must be condemned by Englishmen who see in him only a man who swerved from the ideal height of unimpassioned serenity under circumstances of great difficulty.' *The Times* called Gordon's execution 'excusable homicide' if not 'justifiable homicide.'

However fitting or fair this epitaph might have been, it was premature. Having again failed to secure a warrant for murder against Edward Eyre, the Jamaica Committee decided to revert to its plan of the previous year: it would try to have the former Governor indicted for high crimes and misdemeanours under the Colonial Governors Act. By April, the Jamaica Committee had fully prepared its case along the new lines and Sir Robert Collier had convinced another Bow Street magistrate, Vaughn, to issue a warrant for Eyre for 'having issued an illegal and oppressive proclamation, and caused diverse illegal acts to be committed under the same; and, further, with having unlawfully caused the arrest, imprisonment, and flogging of diverse persons resident in the island of Jamaica, by virtue of the said illegal proclamation of martial law issued by him.' On May 15th, the hearing before Magistrate Vaughn resumed. Besides the immediate participants, there were scarcely more than a dozen persons in the courtroom, the public appearing, for the moment, to have tired of the Jamaica prosecutions. Collier launched into a detailed description of the atrocities and produced witnesses to substantiate his statements.

When his turn came, Hardinge Giffard declared that these witnesses were 'in the pay of the Jamaica Committee.' (Some Jamaicans, brought over to testify, had had living expenses paid by Shaen and Roscoe, the Committee's solicitors.) His client, Giffard continued, had been subjected to innumerable prosecutions and, in effect, if not in point of law, Governor Eyre was being prosecuted for an offence for which both he and others had already been tried. Furthermore, Giffard demanded, by what right had the Jamaica Committee usurped the role of public prosecutor? Why, why was there no sympathy expressed for the twenty-eight white victims, men, women, and children, who had been killed by the rebels? While, doubtlessly, excesses had been committed, could Governor Eyre be held responsible for every act on the island? Mill and Taylor had maintained that they only wished to settle the points of law involved in the case, not to punish individuals. If that were the case, they could have attempted to obtain a declaratory act from parliament—after all, the Jamaica Committee was well represented in the House of Commons. But this did not suit them; it would not give them the 'opportunity of parading their statements as to the floggings and hangings and alleged acts of oppression in newspaper reports.' Nor would they be afforded the chance of 'exciting the public and promoting subscriptions—'. At this point, Sir Robert Collier objected to the maligning of his clients, and a short while afterwards Giffard resumed his chair.

Soon after the conclusion of Giffard's remarks, Magistrate Vaughn announced that he felt it to be his duty to commit former Governor Eyre for trial at the Court of Queen's Bench. Turning to the defendant, the Judge solemnly asked if he had anything to say on his own behalf, cautioning him that he should not say anything which might hereafter be used in evidence against him. Edward Eyre rose slowly, and with evident emotion, addressed the court. 'I have only this to say,' he began, 'that not upon me, but upon those who brought me here, lies the foul disgrace that a public servant, who has faithfully discharged his duty for upwards of twenty years, has been now, after two years and a half of persecution, brought to a criminal court and committed for trial for having performed his duty at a trying moment, and thereby saved, indubitably, a great British colony from destruction, and its well-disposed inhabitants, white and black, from massacre or worse.' The courtroom spectators burst into spontaneous applause. Magistrate Vaughn called for order. Eyre continued. 'I do not envy the feelings of those who, having first conspired to bring me and my family to ruin, have now succeeded in branding me with the additional stigma of a criminal prosecution; but I have this consolation, I rejoice in thinking that my conduct has been impugned only by a small and unimportant section of the community, and that the decision of this Court will not be accepted by the higher tribunal to which the case has been referred. I am satisfied that the large majority of my fellow-countrymen do not sanction these proceedings against me, and to their sense of justice, and to their common sense, I may say, I confidently intrust my honour as a gentleman and my character as a public officer. I have nothing further to say.' The courtroom rang with cheering.

Eyre had again demonstrated that when he spoke—he had spoken but rarely since his return—he could attract sympathy. In the days following his committal for trial, many who claimed to have been hitherto uncommitted, sent cheques to the Eyre Committee, citing Eyre's courtroom speech as the reason for their action. The commitment of Eyre for trial before the grand jury of Queen's Bench again revived lagging interest in the Jamaica case, as had Eyre's eloquent address to the court. The case of Governor Eyre again became a chief topic of discussion in the press. Exeter Hall speakers began anew to denounce the 'wholesale murderer' and the Governor's supporters were once more eulogizing 'the saviour of Jamaica.'

The revival of interest in the Jamaica controversy was reflected in parliament, where the Conservative M.P. for Harwich, Colonel H. J. W. Jervis, a prominent member of the Eyre Defence Committee, rose to ask the new prime minister, Benjamin Disraeli, who had succeeded to that office after the death of the Earl of Derby, whether the Government would undertake to defend Eyre or would it allow him to remain dependent upon 'subscriptions raised through the medium of advertisements in the newspapers.' 'Was it to be understood,' Jervis went on, 'that any man undertaking the government of a colony would in future have to fall back on public charity for his defence should he be placed in a felon's dock for trial?' It was not easy for the Prime Minister to answer. Many Conservative M.P.'s were staunch members of the Eyre Committee and naturally sought to enlist the full support of their party for the ex-Governor. One of Disraeli's oldest friends, Lord John Manners, a son of the Duke of Rutland, for example, was deeply aroused by the Eyre case and pressed the Tories to take up the defence of the Governor as a party issue. But other leading Tories—men such as Sir Stafford Northcote, and a former Colonial Secretary, the Earl of Carnarvon—objected, and the Prime Minister found himself in the middle of this cross-fire. Disraeli's reply was that the government would consider all the evidence produced at the trial and if, after it was over, the government believed it right to do so, it would propose that former Governor Eyre be indemnified for his defence. Colonel Jervis was thoroughly dissatisfied with this answer, and so was a good part of the Tory press. The most frequent refrain was 'Oh, how differently Palmerston would have behaved were he now Prime Minister!'

The Jamaica Committee's decision to prosecute Eyre for high crimes and misdemeanours brought Charles Buxton back into the fold. In a letter to John Stuart Mill, he extended his support:

> When the Jamaica Committee decided to prosecute Mr Eyre on charge of murder, I withdrew from it partly on the ground that I did not consider that Mr Eyre's acts, however outrageous, amounted to murder; and, secondly because I thought it would tend to reinstate Mr Eyre in public opinion, and have in every way a disastrous effect if an unsuccessful attempt were made to bring him to trial on such a charge.
>
> Neither of those objections apply to the course now taken by the Committee. . . .

He enclosed a cheque for £300. This was one of the few pleasant items which the morning's mail brought to Mill during the weeks preceding Eyre's trial. The chairman of the Jamaica Committee became the target of cranks who objected to his 'persecution' of Governor Eyre. One of them addressed his letter to 'The Mill atheist of Westminster, lately M.P., but now a dog.' Another, more temperate, wrote: 'John, your conduct is vindictive, malicious and disgraceful.' A third threatened to stab Mill to death. Writing to Goldwin Smith, Mill reported: 'I receive abusive letters at the rate of three or four a week, and the other day I received one threatening me with assassination. They are all anonymous, and as ineffably stupid as one might expect.' The worst of the business for Mill was that it indicated 'the spirit of our higher classes and of a considerable portion of the public.'

In a letter, dated 30th May 1868, Goldwin Smith reported the entire business to an American friend. 'I don't know whether you have followed the case,' Smith wrote, describing the legal action against Eyre; 'the charge was dismissed some time ago by a bench of Tory county magistrates the exact counterparts of your Southern "aristocrats." There I thought the case would end; but our lawyers now think that they can get at Eyre in another way; and though the state of opinion among the upper class, from which our Grand Juries are taken, is such as scarcely to leave us any hope of success, the Jamaica Committee, with Mill at their head, think it their duty to the country to exhaust all possible modes of obtaining justice for the subject races and wiping off the stain from the national honour. I feel bound to see this out, more especially as Mill and Taylor, in whose names the prosecution is carried on, are the objects of the fiercest odium on the part of the whole upper-class mob and Mill even receives threats of assassination. Probably, however, the end will come on Tuesday next, when a Grand Jury will almost certainly ignore the Bill in face of the Judge's charge, however decided the charge may be. The Eyre party threaten counter-prosecution for conspiracy; but their threats are idle, every educated and decently impartial judge before whom we have gone having recognised the existence of sufficient ground for the proceedings; though I really believe if a bench of county magistrates and Grand Jurymen had to decide our fate, there is nothing of which, in their present temper, they would not find us guilty. Plutocracy styling itself aristocracy, has displayed its character in this affair with a distinctness which is really fearful.'

On 2nd June 1868, the case of the Queen vs. Edward John Eyre went before the Grand Jury of Queen's Bench. On this occasion, Mr Justice Colin Blackburn was entrusted with the task of delivering the charge. Blackburn, unlike his senior colleague, Sir Alexander Cockburn, did not generally have the opportunity of sitting in judgment in sensational cases, although, during the previous October, he had presided over the trial of the Manchester Fenians. But, no doubt, the day when he delivered his charge to the Grand Jury in the case of Governor Eyre, was the most celebrated moment of his judicial career. Blackburn did not possess Cockburn's flash or brilliant legal style—although most of the legal profession believed him more learned in the law. Nor was his reading of the charge as filled with drama or with pomp and ceremony as Cockburn's had been the preceding year. His presentation took a bare two hours, but, in later years, in the realm of high constitutional argument, it was to be regarded as highly, and to be quoted as frequently, as the charge of the Chief Justice.

In lucid fashion, Justice Blackburn took the Grand Jury over thorny questions of British constitutional law. He discussed whether Jamaica was to be regarded as a 'conquered' colony where the law of England did not necessarily apply or a 'settled' colony, where it did; the extent of the powers of the Jamaica legislature; the power of the Crown to proclaim martial law, and so on. After much winding analysis, the Justice concluded that by maintaining martial law for thirty days after all armed resistance had been put down in only a day or two, Governor Eyre had exceeded by much the most extended view of the powers of the Crown (although he felt that, in dealing with insurrection or foreign invasion, the Crown might indeed have the power to proclaim and enforce martial law). However, the law of England transferred to

Jamaica at the time of settlement had been completely altered by the Jamaica statutes, and a much more extended power had been given to the Governor of Jamaica than had ever been possessed by the Crown in Great Britain. On the point of law, therefore, the Governor of Jamaica, acting with the consent of a Council of War, *did* have the right to proclaim martial law under special circumstances and that, once proclaimed, that state of martial law was to remain in force for thirty days.

The Grand Jury had to decide upon the questions of fact, the Justice declared. The first was whether, given the disturbances at Morant Bay, Governor Eyre was justified in proclaiming martial law—and Blackburn felt that if he had not done so he would have been remiss in his duty. The next, whether Eyre was punishable for not having stopped martial law before the thirty-day period had expired. The jurors must place themselves in Governor Eyre's position, mindful of the information which he had before him, and decide what *they* would have done under the circumstances. Another crucial question was whether Eyre was legally justified in arresting Gordon in Kingston, where martial law did not exist, and removing him to Morant Bay, where it did, there to be tried by court martial and executed. The question here was whether the speedy trial and execution of Gordon had helped to stamp out the insurrection, or rather whether a reasonable man would believe that it would help to do so. The evidence pointed to the fact that Gordon was 'a pestilent firebrand,' Blackburn declared. Although he, Blackburn, did not believe that Gordon had been a party to an organized conspiracy to cause an insurrection, nevertheless if Eyre had acted in this manner because he had thought so, then the Governor would have been fully justified in taking the course he did. What would the jurors do in Eyre's place? That was the question which Blackburn put to the Grand Jury, and his description of the conditions surrounding Eyre in October 1865 could only encourage the jurors to the conclusion that any reasonable man would have acted just as the ex-Governor had acted. On the questions of law upon which he had spoken, the Justice, most surprisingly, assured the jurors that he had consulted with all the judges of the Court of Queen's Bench, including the Lord Chief Justice and that they had concurred in his views.

Blackburn then proceeded to go over the counts of the indictment, and, in effect, dismissed every one of them on the basis of the arguments outlined. 'Now, gentlemen,' Blackburn concluded, 'I have done, I think, everything I can to help you in this case.'

You will find, I think, when you come to look at the case, that the great question, and the important question for you, will be carefully to draw your own inference as to what really were the circumstances and position of Jamaica—how things came to Mr Eyre's mind in Jamaica in the very difficult position in which he was, and whether or not there was criminal excess in the sense I have pointed out. The greater part of what I have said latterly is to help and assist you, not to direct you. You will have to determine the question of fact for yourselves upon your own responsibility, I am glad to say it is not mine. . . .

The following day, the foreman of the Grand Jury announced to the Court of Queen's Bench that the jury did not find sufficient grounds for indicting the former governor of Jamaica for high crimes and misdemeanours. The case of the Queen vs. Edward John Eyre was over—Eyre had been acquitted, had been pronounced justified in his conduct by a high court justice and a jury of his peers. The Jamaica Committee had lost once again—just as it had lost at Market Drayton, and in the case of Nelson and Brand. Only this occasion was to be its final and irrevocable defeat.

There remains a postscript to the legal proceedings at the Court of Queen's Bench, a postscript in keeping with the stormy events of the great debate. The controversy which had split both Liberal and Conservative parties, had separated the closest of friends, had created a deep chasm in the world of mid-Victorian letters, was also, even after it had breathed its last in the courts of law, to give rise to a most unusual and undignified squabble between two of Great Britain's highest judges. The altercation was occasioned by Justice Blackburn's statement in his charge that he had consulted with all his brother justices, including the Lord Chief Justice, on the questions of law involved in the case, and that they had concurred. Since Blackburn's statement of the 'law' was so different from that of Cockburn, it appeared that the Lord Chief Justice had either changed his mind or that there had been a misunderstanding. The latter turned out to be the case. Several days after the presentation of the Blackburn charge, the Lord Chief Justice read a statement in court in which he denied absolutely that he had agreed with Blackburn's view of the law. In fact, he took the subordinate justice severely to task for his opinions upon the Jamaica events, in particular for his view of the court martial of George William Gordon.

EPILOGUE

Now that the case was over, Englishmen took stock. The significance of the controversy in terms of constitutional law, imperial relationships, and domestic politics was explored once more—very much as it had been earlier. Liberal magazines and newspapers again asked themselves why it was that the British public had given its sympathy to ex-Governor Eyre rather than to Mill and the Jamaica Committee. Even the most rabid of the Radical papers had no doubt but that the gentlemen justices at Market Drayton, and the two London grand juries had expressed the views of the overwhelming majority of the British middle classes.

The Liberal weekly, *Spectator*, published a lengthy analysis of this question in early June of 1868. 'The upper and middle class of the English people,' the *Spectator* declared, '*especially* the latter . . . are positively enraged at the demand of negroes for equal consideration with Irishmen, Scotchmen, and Englishmen.' It added: 'proceedings which would have cost the most well-meaning of weak-judging men his head if they had taken place in the United Kingdom—which would have been received with shouts of execration if they had taken place in France or Austria—are heartily admired as examples of "strong government" when they take place in the British West Indies.' This was the opinion of nine tenths of the nation, the weekly asserted. At least this percentage was convinced that Negroes ought not to expect the same treatment as Anglo-Saxons, or even Celts. 'We pardon Eyre,' the paper continued, 'because his error of judgment involves only negro blood, what would have otherwise been in our nation's eyes simply unpardonable. We not only pardon him, but positively *howl* at every one who wishes to sustain the tradition of British impartiality, and of recognized ministerial responsibility for these grave aberrations of judgment. . . . The word used against those who try to sustain the higher doctrine of government is "persecution." The motives attributed to them are motives of pure malice. For our own parts,' the *Spectator* solemnly concluded, 'we view the spirit in which this prosecution has been treated by the nation generally, with sincere shame. It shows, we believe, that a partial, a vulgar, and an insolent temper still lurks in our hearts, utterly inconsistent with the equity, magnanimity, and self-restraint needful to a people wielding a great empire which they can only extend by moral and religious virtues of a high order, and which they cannot lose without bringing down anarchy upon the earth.' The *Spectator* did not choose to discuss Ruskin's accusation that the Radicals, by their simultaneous denunciation of Eyre's treatment of Jamaica Negroes and neglect of the dismal condition of English workmen, had revealed themselves to be hypocrites.

The friends of Governor Eyre were jubilant and unrepentant, and exulted in his legal vindication. But they wished to obtain his complete rehabilitation—in specific terms, this meant the payment of his legal expenses by the government and his restoration to the colonial service. The first effort towards rehabilitation came on the 9th of June, just a few days after the decision of the grand jury. A Conservative supporter of Eyre asked Disraeli, on the floor of the House of Commons, whether the Government would now move to defray Eyre's legal expenses. Disraeli responded by stating that the Government had already written to Eyre for a listing of his expenses, which it promised to consider. At the same time a petition was presented to the government which requested the early reappointment of Eyre to a position of responsibility in the colonies. According to the petition's circulators, it contained over 10,000 signatures. Eyre supporters in the House of Commons boasted of 'The vast preponderance of opinion' in favour of Eyre 'among the educated and enlightened classes of the community, and especially among those who know anything about the colonies.' After his acquittal by the grand jury, the ex-Governor's friends organized an 'Eyre Testimonial Fund'—the need for defence having vanished—to provide a nest-egg for their pensionless, jobless hero. Some thousands of pounds were reported to have been collected. But nothing further was done about either defraying Eyre's legal expenses or employing the Governor during the remaining months of the Conservative Government. An election was approaching, and the issue was an explosive one, especially among the newly enfranchised working classes who would vote for the first time.

The election provided an opportunity for the Governor's friends to seek vengeance for the previous three years of 'persecution.' They concentrated their venom upon the chairman of the Jamaica Committee, John Stuart Mill, and devoted their energies to securing his defeat at Westminster. They succeeded. The philosopher and economist was destined to serve only a few brief years in the House of Commons. Every constituency in the area of metropolitan London elected a Liberal M.P. in this election of 1868—every constituency, that is, but Westminster where Mill was crushingly defeated by the Tory, over whom he had scored his victory three years earlier. On the afternoon of the day of the election, an old friend met Sir Roderick Murchison in the street. The gentleman-geologist's first words were about the polls. When Murchison's friend predicted that Mill would probably be defeated, the old man rubbed his hands in delight. 'I was out by eight o'clock this morning to vote against him,' he said. 'I would walk the shoes off my old feet to have the fellow turned out after his infamous conduct towards Governor Eyre.'

But although the friends of the Governor had had their revenge against Mill, the other leaders of the Jamaica Committee had been successful. The first fruits of Reform

were apparent in the size of the vote—and in the size of
the Liberal majority. Some 2,290,000 votes were cast. The
Liberals received over 1,400,000 of them while the Conservatives only garnered about 880,000. Tom Hughes had
been elected once more, although this time for Frome
instead of Lambeth. Peter Taylor had been re-elected.
Among the ministers of the new Liberal Government,
headed by William Gladstone, were many persons with
whom we have become familiar in the course of our story.
Most prominently placed was John Bright, who entered
the Cabinet as the President of the Board of Trade. George
Otto Trevelyan, who had composed the doggerel verse
about Kingsley at Southampton, was made a Junior Lord
of the Admiralty. Sir Robert Collier, who had served as
the Jamaica Committee's barrister in its last unsuccessful
prosecution of Eyre, was named Attorney-General.

In 1869, a series of civil suits for damages was brought
against Eyre by victims of the Jamaica insurrection—the
men who had been imprisoned and flogged and whose
homes and property had been destroyed. Eyre's defence—
that the Act of Indemnity passed by the Jamaica Legislature specifically exempted him from all financial responsibility in connection with the suppression of the insurrection—was, however, upheld by the courts.

The curtain was not rung down upon the Jamaica affair
until July 1872—over four years after the grand jury had
voted to throw the Eyre case out of court. During the
spring of 1872, the Liberal government of William Ewart
Gladstone had declined to consider granting Edward Eyre
either a pension or another appointment, but acknowl-
edged that the possibility of defraying the former governor's legal expenses was under consideration. It was on
this question of legal expenses that a full-scale debate
took place in the House of Commons in July. The inter-
vening years had not diminished the intensity of feelings.
Colonel North, the rabid old Tory from Oxfordshire who
had served in the House for over twenty years, was as
active in defending Eyre as he had been in 1866 and
1867. Also speaking on behalf of the ex-Governor were

Gathorne Hardy, the former Tory Home Secretary who
had protested the Cockburn charge in the summer of
1867, and the former Tory Under-Secretary for the Colonies, Adderley, now Sir Charles Adderley, who had taken
a leading part in the debate of July 1866. John Stuart
Mill had, of course, gone from the House, but the Jamaica
Committee was represented by two of its stalwarts, Peter
Taylor and Thomas Hughes.

The circumstances of the debate were paradoxical. It
was a Liberal government which offered a resolution to
defray Eyre's legal expenses, much to the glee of the Conservatives, and the government was being opposed by its
own Radical wing. It was the over-scrupulousness of William Gladstone which had brought matters to a head. After
reviewing the correspondence which had passed between
Eyre and the Tory government of 1868, Gladstone had
concluded that that Government had in fact promised to
pay the ex-Governor's legal expenses. Therefore, the
Liberal government of 1872 would fulfill the commitment
made by the Tory government of 1868. The Radicals and
Dissenters were furious. The entire controversy was resur-
rected. On the day set aside for the debate, handbills,
signed by prominent trade union leaders, had been distributed to the members of the House. The handbills,
reminiscent of those which deluged London during the
years of the affair, recounted the atrocities committed by
the British authorities and denounced all attempts to grant
even a penny to the 'murderer' Eyre. A practical question
entered the debate. There had, after all, been a fund to
raise money for Eyre's defence and it was commonly understood—although no one was certain—that the Eyre Defence Fund had collected about £13,000, and in addition,
the Eyre Testimonial Fund had raised some £3,000. Together, both funds had collected about four times the
amount that Eyre claimed for legal expenses. If the
government undertook to pay for Eyre's defence under
these circumstances, the Radicals argued, would this not
be interpreted as a testimonial for the Governor, and indication of official approval of his actions?

One Radical M.P., who appeared to have forgotten the

failure of the suits of Jamaicans who *had* come to England
to seek redress, asserted that if Gordon had not been put
to death but had merely been given some minor punishment, he could have come to England, sued Eyre for
damages and would almost certainly have received them;
but 'because instead of being merely flogged, Mr Gordon
had been put to death, and a verdict could not be obtained against Mr Eyre owing to legal technicalities, the
public was asked to pay all his legal expenses!' This would
be misunderstood, the speaker warned, by the public and
'especially by the working classes' who 'were watching this
debate with keen interest.' Charles Gilpin, a long-time antagonist of Eyre and a former member of the Jamaica
Committee Executive, told the members of the House that
'there were still men in this country who deemed that the
proper position of a Briton was to have his foot on the
neck of somebody, and if that somebody possessed a skin
not coloured like his own, then that foot should rest the
heavier and the weightier.' The Governor's defenders were
again—as in July 1866, eight years before—led by Adderley
who proclaimed Eyre a loyal public servant who had been
treated with 'cruel injustice,' by the now defunct Jamaica
Committee, a Committee full of 'Abolitionists, who were
in sympathy with the Baptists in the island, and they did
not think anything could justify the execution of a Baptist.'

It was already past the dinner hour and some hungry
members called for a vote on the resolution. But speaker
followed speaker and the time for voting seemed far off
as the debate droned on repetitiously. It is to Peter Taylor,
the former Treasurer of the Jamaica Committee, to whom
we shall assign the last word. 'Sir,' Taylor began, 'I cannot
but think that the Government have adopted a most unwise course in this matter. The motion cannot but be most
unwelcome to many members of the Government itself,
for if I recollect aright some members of the Government
were actually members of the Jamaica Committee.' Taylor warned of the consequences of a vote in favour of the
motion by members whose constituencies were 'large and
populous.' The workingmen of England would call them
to account. Taylor left this last testament concerning the

work of the Jamaica Committee: 'Sir, when these occurrences took place in Jamaica, a very great feeling of
indignation and shame pervaded the great mass of the
population of this country, and a number of gentlemen
constituted themselves a committee who should be the
representatives of that great feeling of indignation and
shame. The Jamaica Committee thought it their bounden
duty—a duty they owed to justice and humanity, and that
they believed they owed to the honour of their country—
to bring these transactions within the purview and before
a high Court of Law in this country that they might know
authoritatively, whether the deeds done in Jamaica were
legal and justifiable or not.' In Britain's imperial history,
there had occurred many unhappy events. 'We have been
violent, cruel, tyrannical.' But there was usually some palliative, some excuse. For instance, in India 'there was the
courage, devotion, chivalry of a small body of men pitted
against a whole host of barbarians.' In Jamaica, 'there is
neither excuse nor palliative.' The case of Jamaica 'is a
case of cowardice which magnified a trumpery riot into
a widespread insurrection, and then drowned the phantom
it created in an ocean of murder, anarchy, and blood.'

Taylor's concluding remarks were both a confession of
failure and, at the same time, a triumphant shout of success: 'I have defended to the best of my poor ability the
acts of the Jamaica Committee. I have not a word of
apology to make, not a word of apology to utter. Were
the case to occur again, I would endeavour again to bring
the actor to the bar of his country. The hypothesis is needless, for it will never occur again. The Jamaica Committee,
failing in all its direct aims, and almost overwhelmed amid
a storm of obloquy and misrepresentation have done their
work—have fulfilled their mission; they have stamped out
a policy. Never again in a British colony—whatever may
be the result of the contemptible vote of to-night—never
again in a British Colony shall be enacted the policy of
ex-Governor Eyre, nor the world stand aghast at the atrocities of a Jamaica massacre.'

The result of the 'contemptible vote' was as Taylor must
have anticipated. Ayes, those in favour of having the Gov-

ernment defray Eyre's legal expenses, 243. Noes, 130. Upon hearing this, John Stuart Mill became angry, and declared that never again would he vote for a Liberal government. Mill died the following year, 1873, a year before the election which saw the Conservative government of Benjamin Disraeli swept back into office. In their first year of office, the Tories voted to grant Edward Eyre a pension as a 'retired' colonial governor.

It would be satisfying to report that Peter Taylor's faith in the future was justified, that, as a result of the efforts of the Jamaica Committee, 'never again in a British colony' was there 'enacted the policy of ex-Governor Eyre,' and never again did 'the world stand aghast at the atrocities of a Jamaica massacre.' It was not to be so. The Jamaica reign of terror of 1865 which had helped to crystallize the contending arguments and the lines of battle between those who placed empire foremost and those who thought first of liberty, was one of the first, but hardly the last of the administrative massacres by means of which European nations strove to keep vast empires. The controversies which had been so dramatically raised by the Jamaica affair were to be waged again and again in the years to come, even until the present day.

The issue of martial law was once more to become a subject of public controversy during the Boer War, the war against the two independent republics in South Africa which Britain waged between 1899 and 1901. The Boer cause was championed by the same groups which had constituted the Jamaica Committee—by the Radicals, grown stronger and more numerous in both the country and in parliament, and by the non-conformists. The war proved to be a lengthy and a difficult one and the Tory Government felt obliged to turn to martial law. The Radicals protested. Many of the actors in the Jamaica drama of thirty-five years previously were still on the political stage. (Edward Eyre, for example, was still alive—he died in 1901. His last years were spent out of the public eye, supported by his pension.) The legality of martial law in South Africa was publicly questioned by the now septua-

genarian Frederic Harrison who again declared that it
opened the way 'to anarchy and horrible reprisals' and
that 'no more momentous peril to law and order had
arisen for centuries.' Harrison was supported in his position
by another Jamaica Committee stalwart, the greatest English philosopher of the day, Herbert Spencer. Both Harrison and Spencer invoked the already half-forgotten charge
delivered by Lord Chief Justice Cockburn to support their
claims. It seemed poetically appropriate that the legality
of martial law should have been re-affirmed at this time
by the Lord Chancellor of England, the Earl of Halsbury,
who was Hardinge Giffard, Edward Eyre's barrister of
nearly four decades earlier.

What had seemed so extraordinary to John Stuart Mill
and his comrades—administrative massacre, rule by terror
—has become a commonplace in the imperial history of
our century: Amritsar, the Black and Tans in Ireland,
Cyprus, Nyasaland. The War of 1939 brought the tech-
nique into operation once more against non-colonial,
European peoples. It is dreadful to think that the forces
at play in 1865 may have helped to set into motion our
own greater calamities. Race prejudice—the view that
what might be considered an outrage if committed against
a white people could go unnoticed if committed against
an 'inferior' coloured people was the principle underlying
the acceptance of the deeds of Governor Eyre and of
Colonel Nelson by the British public. As we now see, it
was a principle capable of indefinite extension in all
directions.

The essential question was whether a nation could long
maintain two contradictory policies, democracy at home
and repression and terror abroad. Great Britain managed
to maintain the distinction between domestic liberty and
imperial authority for over a century. She had geography
in her favour. Democracy triumphed in Great Britain even
while she presided—in well-nigh absolute fashion—over
hundreds of millions of coloured colonial subjects overseas.
Yet, in the larger sense, the Radicals were correct in their
view that either the terms under which the empire was

held were bound to change the character of the British constitution or the spirit of the constitution was bound to change the character of the Empire. The latter course, fortunately, prevailed, and the result is a Commonwealth composed of all races, enjoying the benefits of association along with independence. Perhaps the Jamaica Committee deserves some share of credit for this transformation, and for steadfastly proclaiming the great truth that liberty is a seamless garment, that, to paraphrase Frederic Harrison's statement on English law, it is that kind of intangible, which, if you play fast and loose with it, vanishes.

SELECTED BIBLIOGRAPHY

*The Times**   *Economist*
The Manchester Guardian   *Fortnightly Review*
News of the World   *Fraser's*
      Illustrated London News
Annual Register   *Macmillan's*
Parliamentary Debates   *Punch*
Parliamentary Papers   *Saturday Review*
      Spectator

Athenaeum
Blackwoods   *Dictionary of National*
Cornhill   *Biography*

Goldwin Smith Papers. University Archives. Cornell University. New York.

Abrahams, Peter. *Jamaica; An Island Mosaic*. London: Her Majesty's Stationery Office, 1957.

Bodelsen, C. A. G. *Studies in Mid-Victorian Imperialism*. Kopenhagen: Gyldendalske Boghandel, 1924.

Bright, John. *The Public Letters of the Right Hon. John Bright, M. P.* London: S. Low et al., 1885.

Burns, Sir Alan. *History of the British West Indies*. London: Allen & Unwin, 1954.

The Times was especially useful in piecing together the day-to-day events of the Controversy.

Buxton, Charles. *Reply to Mr Charles Buxton to Certain Electors of East Surrey.* London?: 1866.

Carlyle, Alexander, (ed.) *Letters of Thomas Carlyle to J. S. Mill, John Sterling and Robert Browning.* London: T. F. Unwin, 1923.

Carlyle, Alexander. *New Letters of Thomas Carlyle.* London: J. Lane, 1904.

Carlyle, Jane Welsh. *Letters and Memorials of J. W. Carlyle.* New York: G. Munro, 1883.

Chamerovzow, L. A. *Borneo Facts versus Borneo Fallacies.* London, 1849.

Cockburn, Sir Alexander. *Charge of the Lord Chief Justice of England to the Grand Jury at the Central Criminal Court, in the Case of the Queen against Nelson & Brand.* London: W. Ridgway, 1867.

Collingwood, W. G. *The Life and Work of John Ruskin.* Boston: Houghton Mifflin, 1893.

Cook, E. J. *The Life of John Ruskin.* New York: Macmillan, 1911.

Courtney, W. L. *Life of J. S. Mill.* London: W. Scott, 1889.

Cox, Homersham. *A History of the Reform Bills of 1866 and 1867.* London: Longmans, Green, 1868.

Curtin, Philip D. *Two Jamaicas: The role of ideas in a tropical colony, 1830–1865.* Cambridge: Harvard University Press, 1955.

Dangerfield, George. *Bengal mutiny; the story of the Sepoy Rebellion.* New York: Harcourt, Brace, 1933.

Darwin, Francis. *The Life and Letters of Charles Darwin.* New York: D. Appleton, 1887.

Dickens, Charles. *Miscellaneous Papers.* London: Chapman and Hall, 1908.

Duncan, David, (ed.) *Life and Letters of Herbert Spencer.* New York: D. Appleton, 1908.

Elliot, Hugh S. R. (ed.) *The Letters of J. S. Mill.* London: Longmans, Green, 1910.

Evans, J., and Whitehouse, J. H. *The Diaries of John Ruskin.* Oxford: Clarendon Press, 1958.

Everett, Edwin M. *The Party of Humanity: The Fort-

nightly Review and Its Contributors (1865–1874).
Chapel Hill: University of North Carolina Press, 1939.

Eyre, Edward John. *Journals of expeditions of discovery into Central Australia.* London: 1845.

Finlason, W. F. *Commentaries upon Martial Law.* London: Stevens & Sons, 1867.

——. *The History of the Jamaica Case.* London: Chapman & Hall, 1869.

——. *Justice to a Colonial Governor; or, Some considerations on the case of Mr Eyre.* London: Chapman & Hall, 1868.

——. *Report of the Case of the Queen v. Edward John Eyre, on his prosecution, in the Court of Queen's Bench.* London: Chapman & Hall, 1868.

Froude, J. A. *The English in the West Indies.* London: 1885.

——. *Thomas Carlyle; a history of his life in London, 1834–1881.* London: Longmans, Green, 1884.

Geikie, Sir Archibald. *Life of Sir Roderick Impey Murchison.* London, 1875.

Hall, S. C. *Retrospect of a Long Life, from 1815 to 1883.* London, 1883.

Harrison, Frederic. *Autobiographic Memoirs.* London: Macmillan, 1911.

——. *Martial Law, Six letters to 'The Daily News.'* London: The Jamaica Committee, 1867.

Himmelfarb, Gertrude. *Darwin and the Darwinian Revolution.* London: Chatto & Windus, 1959.

Hirst, F. W. *The Early Life and Letters of John Morley.* London: Macmillan, 1927.

Hodder, Edwin. *Life of Samuel Morley.* London: Hodder & Stoughton, 1887.

Hume, A. H. *The Life of Edward John Eyre, late Governor of Jamaica.* London: R. Bentley, 1867.

Huxley, Leonard. *Life and Letters of Thomas Henry Huxley,* London: 1900.

Irvine, William. *Apes, Angels, and Victorians.* New York: McGraw Hill, 1955.

Jamaica Committee. *Jamaica Papers.* Nos. 1–3 (1866).

Johnson, Edgar. *Charles Dickens: His Tragedy and Triumph*. New York: Simon and Schuster, 1952.

Kemper, Else. 'Carlyle as Imperialist,' *Zeitschrift für Politik*, XI (1918), pp. 115–166.

Kingsley, Mrs C. *Charles Kingsley: His Letters and Memories of His Life*. London: 1891.

Leon, Derrick. *Ruskin, the Great Victorian*. London: Routledge, and Kegan Paul, 1949.

Lippincott, B. E. *Victorian Critics of Democracy: Carlyle, Ruskin, Arnold, Stephen, Maine, Lecky*. Minneapolis: The University of Minnesota Press, 1938.

Low, Sidney. *The History of England During the Reign of Victoria (1857–1901)*. London: Longmans, Green, 1911.

McCarthy, Justin. *A History of Our Own Times*. London: Chatto & Windus, 1878.

McDonnell, W. *Exeter Hall: A Theological Romance*. London, 1869.

Marindin, G. E., (ed.) *Letters of Frederic Lord Blachford, Under-secretary of State for the Colonies, (1860–1871)*. London: John Murray, 1896.

Marriott, Sir J. A. R. *England Since Waterloo*. London: Methuen, 1936.

Marx, Karl and Engels, Friedrich. *Briefwechsel*. Berlin: Dietz Verlag, 1950.

Mathieson, W. L. *The Sugar Colonies and Governor Eyre, 1849–1866*. London: Longmans, Green, 1936.

Mill, J. S. *Autobiography*. London, 1874.

———. *Dissertations and Discussions*. London: 1875.

Monypenny, W. F., and Buckle, G. E. *The Life of Benjamin Disraeli, Earl of Beaconsfield*. London: John Murray, 1929.

Neff, E. E. *Carlyle and Mill*. New York: Columbia University Press, 1926.

Olivier, Margaret. *Sydney Olivier; Letters and Selected Writings*. London: Allen & Unwin, 1948.

Olivier, Sydney. *The Myth of Governor Eyre*. London: L. & V. Woolf, 1933.

Packe, Michael S. J. *Life of John Stuart Mill*. London: Secker & Warburg, 1954.

Paul, Herbert. *A History of Modern England.* London: Macmillan, 1904–1906.

Price, George. *Jamaica and the Colonial Office: Who caused the crisis?* London: The Author, 1866.

Reid, T. W. *Life of the Right Honourable William Edward Forster.* London: Chapman & Hall, 1888.

Ruskin, John. *The Works of John Ruskin,* Cook, E. T., and Wedderburn, A., (eds.) London: George Allen, 1903–1912.

Russell, G. W. E. *Letters of Matthew Arnold, 1848–1888.* London, 1900.

Schapiro, J. Salwyn. *Liberalism and the Challenge of Fascism.* New York: McGraw-Hill, 1949.

Semmel, Bernard. *Imperialism and Social Reform.* London: Allen & Unwin, 1960.

——. 'The Philosophic Radicals and Colonialism,' in *The Journal of Economic History,* December 1961.

Sewell, W. G. *The Ordeal of Free Labour in the British West Indies.* New York: Harper & Brothers, 1861.

Smith, Goldwin. *The Civil War in America: An Address read at the last meeting of the Manchester Union and Emancipation Society.* London, 1866.

——. *Reminiscences.* New York: Macmillan, 1910.

——. *Three English Statesmen: a course of lectures on the political history of England.* London: Macmillan, 1867.

Spencer, Herbert. *An Autobiography.* London: Williams & Norgate, 1904.

Stephen, Leslie. *The English Utilitarians.* London: Duckworth, 1900.

——. *The Life of Sir James Fitzjames Stephen.* London: Smith, Elder, 1895.

Tennyson, *Alfred Lord Tennyson, A Memoir* [by his son] London: Macmillan, 1897.

Torrens, W. T. McC. *Twenty Years in Parliament.* London: R. Bentley, 1893.

Trevelyan, G. M. *British History in the 19th Century and After, 1782–1919.* London: Longmans, 1947.

——. *Life of John Bright.* London: Constable, 1925.

Trevelyan, Sir George Otto. *The Ladies in Parliament and Other Pieces.* Cambridge: 1869.

Trilling, Lionel. *Matthew Arnold*. New York: Columbia University Press, 1949.

Underhill, Edward Bean. *Dr Underhill's Letter. A letter addressed to the Rt Honourable E. Cardwell, with illustrative documents on the condition of Jamaica*. London: A Miall, 1865.

———. *Life of James Mursell Phillippo, Missionary in Jamaica*. London: Yates & Alexander, 1887.

———. *The Tragedy of Morant Bay*. London: Alexander & Shepheard, 1895.

———. *The West Indies: Their social and religious condition*. London: Jackson et al., 1862.

Uren, M. J. L., and Stephens, M. *Waterless Horizons; the first full-length study of the extraordinary life-story of Edward John Eyre, explorer, overlander and pastoralist in Australia*. Melbourne: Robertson & Mullens, 1941.

Whibley, Charles. *Lord John Manners and his friends*. Edinburgh: Blackwood, 1925.

Williams, Benjamin Thomas. *The Case of George William Gordon*. London: 1866.

Wilson, D. A. *Carlyle*. London: K. Paul, Trench, 1923–34.

Wilson-Fox. *The Earl of Halsbury, Lord High Chancellor, 1823–1921*. London: Chapman & Hall, 1929.

Woodward, E. L. *The Age of Reform, 1815–1870*. Oxford: Clarendon Press, 1949.

INDEX

Aborigines Protection Society, 18f.

Adderley, Charles, 78, 82, 184

Anderson, Rev. William, 67

Anti-Slavery Society, 18, 22, 41

Arnold, Matthew, 138, 141

Aspland, Lindsley, 168

Baines, Edward, 68

Baptists, 33, 36, 42, 45, 54, 185

Beales, Edmond, 63, 74, 87ff., 112, 139, 153, 158

Beesly, Professor E. S., 63, 135, 145ff., 153

Blackburn, Justice Colin, 176–179

Boer War, 187

Bogle, Paul, 14, 45–48, 69–70

Brand, Lieutenant Herbert, 53, 55, 77, 150–155, 159, 163, 167, 168ff., 178

Bright, Jacob, 23, 63

Bright, John, 23, 60ff., 66, 72ff., 84, 89, 97, 112, 139, 168, 183

Brooke, Rajah James, 18–19, 21, 105

Buxton, Charles, 65, 66, 72ff., 76ff., 82–83, 150, 168, 174

Buxton, Sir Thomas Fowell, 22, 66, 72

Cairnes, Professor J. E., 63, 67

Canning, 'Clemency', 20

Cardigan, Earl of, 94, 96–97, 121

Cardwell, Edward, 16f., 22, 27, 36, 42–43, 45, 56, 80, 96, 165

Carlyle, Jane, 108, 115

Carlyle, Thomas, 18, 21, 32, 62, 106, 107–127, 130–132, 141, 167

Carnarvon, Earl of, 83–84, 174

Chamerovzow, Louis, 21ff., 41, 157

Chelmsford, Lord, 166

Chesson, F. W., 65

Christian Socialism, 63, 65, 97, 105ff.

Civil War, American, 33, 61–66, 110, 133

Cobden, Richard, 60, 147f.

Cockburn, Sir Alexander, 159–169, 176–179, 188

Collier, Sir Robert, 170ff., 183

Comte, Auguste, 135f.

Cranborne, Lord, 144

Crompton, Henry, 135

Cromwell, Oliver, 32, 110, 124

Crossley, Sir Francis, 66

Daily News, 136

Daily Telegraph, 68, 114, 116

Darwin, Charles, 124–127, 132

Denman, Lord, 166

Dicey, A. V., 123

Dicey, Edward, 63, 68

Dickens, Charles, 120f., 124, 153

Disraeli, Benjamin, 75–76, 82, 105, 144, 173f., 181, 187

Economist, 121, 148

Elcho, Lord, 25, 86f.

Emancipation Society, London and Manchester, 63–65

Engels, Friedrich, 23

Exeter Hall, 17–21, 25f., 56, 62, 64, 71, 107, 110, 121, 145f., 148, 150, 173

Eyre Defence Committee, 28f., 110ff., 115f., 119, 122, 124f., 131f., 156, 173, 184

Eyre, Governor Edward, 11f., 14–17, 22, 24–27, Chapter II, 90–101, 117f., 154–159, 168–173, 183, 186f. And *passim*, throughout.

Eyre, Mary, 23f.

Fawcett, Henry, 23, 123f.

Fenians, 140–141, 144, 147, 153, 165, 176

Forster, W. E., 80, 84, 96, 165

Frankland, Sir Edward, 124

Fraser's Magazine, 18, 109

Froude, J. A., 111

Giffard, Hardinge, 140, 156f., 167, 171f., 188

Gilpin, Charles, 185

Gladstone, W. E., 86, 112, 143f., 183

Gordon, George William, 11, 16, 21, 37–41, 45ff., 52ff., 60, 69ff., 73, 76, 84, 92, 116, 121, 128–129, 132, 136f., 150, 154, 155, 158, 162, 171, 177, 179, 185

Granville, Earl, 160

Green, T. H., 124

Gurney, Samuel, 22, 25, 114

Hardwicke, Earl of, 94, 97–98

Hardy, Gathorne, 165, 183f.

Harrison, Frederic, 135–138, 145, 148, 159, 161, 187f.

Henry, Sir Thomas, 151–152, 154, 170f.

Hobbs, Colonel, 14, 27, 51f., 55, 69, 90

Hooker, Joseph Dalton, 125, 132

Hughes, Thomas, 22, 63–65, 80f., 85, 89, 106, 114, 124, 134, 139, 145, 168, 183f.

Hume, Alexander Hamilton, 28, 110, 113, 118f.

Huxley, Leonard, 12

Huxley, T. H., 123, 125–130, 132ff., 134f., 168

Indian Mutiny, 18ff., 50, 120, 138, 186

Ireland, 140, 142, 144, 146, 165

Jamaica, economic conditions, 31f; religious sects, 33; politics, 33–46, 56–57; Insurrection, 46–55

Jamaica Committee, 64–68, 71–76, 78, 82ff., 89, 91,

Jamaica Committee (*cont'd*)
101f., 122–127, 128, 130,
133, 134, 145, 148, 150ff.,
166–172, 174f., 178, 182,
185–189

Jervis, H. J. W., 173f.

Ketelhodt, Baron von, 35, 39,
45f., 48ff.

Kidd, Benjamin, 127

Kingsley, Charles, 19, 29, 94,
97ff., 101, 104ff., 113, 119,
124, 128f.

Kingsley, Henry, 29f., 98, 104

London Missionary Society, 22

London Workingman's Association, 89

Lowe, Robert, 75, 144

Ludlow, J. M., 63, 106

Lushington, Godfrey, 63, 135

Lyell, Charles, 123ff., 128

Macaulay, Thomas Babington,
20

Manners, Lord John, 174

Maori War, 19f.

Martial Law, 134ff., 154, 162–
166, 176f.

Marx, Karl, 23, 103

Maurice, F. D., 97, 105

McCarthy, Justin, 11f.

Melville, Lord, 26, 166

Miall, Edward, 63, 67, 168

Mill, John Stuart, 18, 61f.,
65f., 67, 72–76, 81f., 85,
88f., 105, 107–110, 112f.,
116, 124, 134f., 139, 143,
147, 152, 167ff., 172, 174f.,
182f., 187f.

Morley, Samuel, 22, 66

Morning Star, 22ff.

Murchison, Sir Roderick,
122f., 182

Nelson, Colonel A. A., 24, 27,
49, 51, 53, 55, 150–155,
159, 163, 167, 168ff., 178,
188

Newman, Professor F. W., 67

News of the World, 22

North, Colonel, 79, 183

Northcote, Sir Stafford, 174

O'Reilly, H. W., 165f.

Pall Mall Gazette, 24, 26,
127f.

Palmerston, Viscount, 19,
58ff., 74, 97, 160, 163, 174

Pearson, Karl, 127

Peterloo Massacre, 142, 147

Peto, Sir Samuel Morton, 66

Positivism, 135f.

Potter, Thomas Bayley, 68,
153

Price, George, 35f., 118

Punch, 25, 146, 157f.

Racism, 18, 79–80, 84, 137f.

Radicalism, 59–68, 80, 116–
117, 120, 125, 147f.

Reform Bill, 59ff., 74f., 143f.;
agitation, 85–90, 100f.,
139f., 143f., 153

Reform League, 85, 87ff., 153,
158

Rogers, Frederic, 16, 31, 36–
37

Rogers, Thorold, 124, 153

Rose, J. Anderson, 155

Rossetti, William, 119

Royal Commission of Inquiry,
27, 68–71, 82, 90, 91, 101,
108, 128

Ruskin, John, 106, 113–123,
124f., 131, 139, 181

Russell, Lord John, 19, 22f.,
74f., 85

Saturday Review, 23

Scott, Benjamin, 67f.

Shaen and Roscoe, 151, 155, 171

Shrewsbury, Earl of, 94, 97

Slack, Henry James, 67

Smith, Goldwin, 64, 124, 175f.

Social-Darwinism, 126

Spectator, 164, 180f.

Spencer, Herbert, 125f., 134, 188

Stephen, J. F., 151–156, 158f., 167, 170

Taylor, Peter, 63, 73f., 152f., 157, 168, 172, 175, 183f., 185f.

Tennyson, Alfred, 120, 124

The Times, 26, 71, 73, 100, 122, 151, 158, 163f., 170f.

Torrens, Robert, 147

Trade Unionism, 63, 65, 135, 145f.

Tramway Scandal, 35f., 118

Trevelyan, G. O., 105 f.n., 183

Tyndall, John, 123, 125, 130–134

Underhill, Edward Bean, 42ff., 54

Vaughan, Magistrate, 171ff.

Volunteers, 25, 47, 122

Wakefield, E. G., 147

Walpole, Sir Spencer, 89